HOME LOVE IT and LEAVE IT

Teenagers' Guide to Surviving the Best/Worst Years of Your Life

David J. Wayne and Nancy N. Rue

Baker Book House

Grand Rapids, Michigan 49506

Copyright 1983 by
Baker Book House Company

ISBN: 0-8010-9662-6

Printed in the United States of America

To our children

Erin
Gavin
Marijean

who will someday
leave home

Contents

1

Leaving Pangs

Whenever a twelve-to-seventeen-year-old person is awake no, make that whenever a teen is breathing—there always seems to be music playing in the background. Some guys can't get through a history chapter without tunes oozing out of their tape decks. There are girls who can't fall asleep unless something mellow is coming from their radios. They can't do the dishes or cruise Main Street or even exist without a beat.

Music is often as much a part of being a teenager as getting a driver's license and eating hamburgers. Think about it if you will. Isn't it an automatic reaction to slide into the car and snap on the radio before the seat belt even goes on? Doesn't a sleepy hand paw at the clock radio before the eyes open in the morning?

Sure, and there's a reason for it. The beat provides a rhythm to work by. Without it, boredom could take over completely! The words can stir up or smooth out a person's feelings. There's a song for just about every question that floats through your mind. Even the harmony—or absence of it—can shape a mood. Whether you wake up to John Denver or Neil Diamond can determine how you feel half the day. For some, music is considered one of the best parts of being a teenager.

But somewhere in the same background those tunes are coming from, there is usually a voice—or maybe a couple of them—calling: "Can't you turn that thing down?" "You call that music?" "How can you understand a thing they're saying?"

Yes, it's the folks, declaring at full volume that the generation gap is still very much with us. With a groan and maybe a little eye-rolling, the defeated teenager brings the tunes to a whisper, changes the station, or turns "that thing" off all together.

There are several reasons, and some of them very sound ones, for believing that a straight diet of rock-and-roll at full volume is unhealthy. We are not suggesting that, on the subject of your music, you are right and your parents are wrong or vice versa. We only mention it here because it is just one of the things that parents and teens do not seem to agree on. We know teens and parents tussle about many other subjects.

When was the last time you put on what "everybody else" is wearing and had to change clothes because mom isn't "everybody else's" mother? Has your father ever ordered you to speak English at the dinner table when you lapsed into the jargon you use at school?

If you got together with five of your friends, you could probably come up with twenty-five subjects you argue with your parents about or avoid talking about at all. It's not that you dislike your parents or think they're not too intelligent. It's just that there are times when you seem to be living on two separate planets.

Yet believe it or not, your folks had pretty much the same feelings when they were fifteen or sixteen. That's hard to fathom when you think of them now, reading the editorial page and struggling over their income tax forms. But they thought and felt the same way every teenager does; like everyone, their attitudes changed sometime after their acne cleared up. No one could convince them when they were suffering through curfews and dress codes that they would ever forget and become "outdated" in the eyes of their own kids, but it happened. It happens to just about everyone.

You see, it is not just growing up in a new and different world that causes a teenager to crave every clothing style, musical group, and slang term parents deplore. It is something else, something that has been going on in every generation since Noah was a kid. It is the first step in the process of "leaving."

Leaving. Leaving home. That idea brings up all kinds of images. For some reason those pictures usually portray a person waking up one morning and suddenly deciding that today is the day to break away. Maybe it's graduation day and you see yourself strolling right from the ceremony into an apartment and a loan on a used car, still wearing cap and gown. Or you feature yourself walking down the aisle on the arm of some strong nine-to-fiver (male or female!) with the feeling that at last you have arrived. You might just envision throwing a radio and some clean jeans into a knapsack and heading for the highway.

Where do we get those ideas anyway? At some point in their childhood most kids get fed up with the rules and toy with the idea of "running away." Some even toss a few peanut-butter sandwiches into a bag and get as far as the next corner. Most turn up at home before they are really missed. But that's where the idea of one day packing it up and hitting the trail first takes shape.

That concept is reinforced by everything from T.V. commercials, where Tommy trots off down the sidewalk at eighteen with a Coke and a smile, to songs in which wailing singers declare they one day "took a ride and never went back." We even hear celebrities—John Wayne to Elton John—explaining on talk shows how they left home at sixteen to go into show business or politics or whatever.

The truth is, leaving starts as more a state of mind than a physical thing. It doesn't just occur the first night someone cooks their first meatloaf in a pan bought that afternoon at

K-Mart. Instead, it is a process, and a long one, that begins years before one is ready to start paying rent.

That thought can be a shocker. Here is another one. At age sixteen most teenagers have been in the process of leaving for two or three years and haven't even realized it. That's because we don't recognize the symptoms of the itch to take off on our own as being that. Those feelings usually masquerade as something else.

The first signs are actually just what we have been talking about. Everybody experiences them. The moment the hair on the back of your neck starts to bristle when your parents criticize your music or your T-shirts or your language is the moment the desire to "leave" begins. From time to time you might seem to be allergic to your parents. You would just as soon hoof the six miles to the gym and meet your friends there for a basketball game as have your folks drive you and let anybody see you reporting what time you will be home. Having your dad drive you and your date anywhere is totally out of the question, and talking on the extension phone in the kitchen with your mom hovering around is worse than not getting a phone call at all, even if the conversation is about something as innocent as the geometry teacher or the agony of eating school lunches.

Again, of course, none of this means a teenage son or daughter really wishes his or her parents would evaporate. It is simply normal. Even the "model" family type teen has those feelings. Take Jennifer, for example.

At fifteen, Jennifer goes on all the family picnics and dutifully laughs at her father's jokes. She even takes out the garbage and keeps her parents posted on her shaky progress in algebra. But she still has those aggravated twinges now and then. She wishes, just for a minute, that her mother would let her pick out her school wardrobe alone this year. As she opens the front door to go out one evening, she gets a sudden burning need to leave the house without giving everyone her proposed minute-by-minute agenda, even though she's only going to the library. She finds herself gritting her teeth every time her father asks if she has done her homework, which of course she has.

Those are just little things in the otherwise serene life of a growing young person. But they represent a healthy desire for some freedom. They do not indicate that Jennifer is likely to climb out her window one night and take off. She is just beginning to see that it might be nice to do some things her own way, now instead of later.

If that process develops as it should, Jennifer will find herself needing to set her own limits. She will confront her parents with the idea of stretching her curfews and dating privileges. She will make some choices alone—like what courses she wants to take next year—and then fill her parents in. As she gets into it all, she will learn when not to agree with everything her parents lay out for her and how to go about telling them painlessly. When it is completed, the process will produce a free, responsible adult woman who probably won't realize it has taken her years to become what she is.

That makes a person want to get cracking on it right away! But let's stop here for a minute and give you a chance to check yourself out on this leaving thing. Are you showing signs that the leaving process has begun? Let's see.

SELF-SURVEY 1

Are You Experiencing Leaving Pangs?

Below you will find some statements about teenagers and their parents. Using the rating scale you see here, decide if and how each one applies to you. Add the ratings for a total at the end.

1   always applies
2   often applies
3   sometimes applies
4   rarely applies
5   never applies

____ a.   My parents give me "unasked-for" advice.

____ b.   I would prefer that my parents knock on my bedroom door before entering.

____ c.   My mother looks through my dresser drawers and other personal belongings when I am not there.

____ d.   I would rather go out with my own friends than participate in family outings.

____ e.   My parents use restriction as a form of discipline.

____ f.   My parents say things like, "How could you do this to me?" or "If you loved us you wouldn't do this" when I do something wrong.

____ g.   My parents call me negative names when they are angry with me.

____ h.   My parents won't talk to me if they are mad at me.

____ i.   When I ask my parents why, they say something like, "Because I said so."

____ j.   My parents and I disagree in our views on such issues as the legalization of marijuana or the death penalty.

____ k.   My parents ask me questions when I come home, such as, "Where have you been?" "Who were you with?" and "Who drove you home?"

____ l.   My parents criticize my choices of things like clothes, hair styles, and music.

____ m.   When I get angry or depressed, my parents say things like, "You shouldn't feel that way."

____ n.   My parents disapprove of my friends.

____ Total

Before we tell you how to score yourself—and before you march up to your parents and announce that, because you break out in a rash when they tell you to set the table, you are on your way to adulthood—let's talk about the other side of the leaving process. It's the flip side to the exciting freedom tune. It's called responsibility.

Take Jon, a sixteen-year-old guy. Jon got himself a part-time job at a fast food place. It is sort of a partial declaration of independence. The money is great. An occasional splurge on a couple of new albums never hurt anybody's morale. But Jon has figured out pretty quickly that there are some strings attached.

A lot is expected on the job. If the fries aren't crisp and he forgets to hold somebody's lettuce and pickle, the boom falls on him—even if he was up until 2:00 a.m. the night before finishing a term paper.

The money doesn't go quite as far as he thought it would either. He has to pay his mom for the gas she's using to cart him back and forth, and since his dad decided Jon should fork over a little cash for his clothes and school supplies now that he's earning an income, there goes another chunk out of the paycheck. Sure, he's breaking away, but he's realizing the break is not as easy as it looked in his daydreams. He starts to have some doubts about making it on his own when he actually graduates and has to support himself the way he plans to. A couple of times he has even found himself thinking back to how simple it was when he was ten and just hunted frogs after school.

Part of the process of leaving, then, is a sort of natural confusion. On one hand, a guy can't wait to cut free and make his own decisions about when to go out, when to come in, what to wear, and how many times a week to go to church. On the other hand, once he gets a glimpse of the hassles that come with that freedom, he starts to wonder if he can handle them or maybe if he even wants to. With all this seesawing back and forth, there is bound to be some tension. That's why there are days when, frankly, a teenager is impossible to live with. (Even for him/herself!)

Most of us don't sit around discussing our feelings the way we do who is dating whom and what old Mr. So-and-So is going to ask on the history exam. Airing your insides to a bunch of your friends sounds like it might be a little uncomfortable. So it is pretty safe to say that average Joe Teenager doesn't tell people he has any kind of turmoil going on inside. It sure doesn't look to him like anyone else feels it, so why make a fool of himself?

Well, here is a flash: Everybody who is a teenager has had

or will have some experience with that confusion. There is not a kid alive who hasn't wondered once or twice if she/he has what it takes to be a success in life. And yet that's the same kid who gets uptight everytime parents give good advice about how to be one!

Knowing you're normal does not automatically make it easier to deal with the whole thing. It's like having bad skin. You are aware that 70 percent of the other kids have it, too, but that doesn't make it any less gruesome to look in the mirror.

Everyone grows out of bad skin eventually, in spite of the number of candy bars and greasy french fries consumed in adolescence. But getting a grip on the confusion—gaining the longed-for freedom and being able to handle the responsibilities that go with it—doesn't just happen with time. There is no magic age at which someone waves goodby over their shoulder and goes out to seek their fortune.

Actually, we are lucky it doesn't happen that way. In many less civilized cultures, young men and women are still initiated into adulthood by what are called "passage rites." At a certain age teenagers are put through an ordeal. If they pass it, they are considered mature adults with all the accompanying rights and privileges. We can count ourselves fortunate when we learn that those ordeals often involve fasting (an impossibility for most adolescent appetites), whipping, and creating designs on the skin with scars. In the Bemba tribe of Africa, they really go all out. A girl must prove her womanhood by catching water insects with her mouth and killing a tethered chicken by sitting on its head! If nothing else, it makes you glad you are an American!

But if we think about it, maybe those folks have the right idea. Rites of passage at the coming of age involve taking young people out of the confusion of society, giving them instruction in social and moral values, and then putting them back into society. Everyone there then says, "Oh, there's Joe. He's been through his initiation. He is an adult now." And then they treat him like one. With his scar design or his shaved scalp, Joe goes about the business of living, knowing he is assured of success. His ordeal has convinced him that he can master his new roles, and the acceptable way to do that is all clear in his head.

In a way, that sounds pretty good. Wouldn't it be great to go through just one period of a few weeks, and come out with all the answers? Wouldn't it be terrific to be able to say, "Hey, you can't treat me that way anymore. I'm an adult now"? It might be worth getting a permanent tattoo and swallowing a few mosquitoes!

But whether we like it or not, no such rites exist in our society. There are reasons for that. One of them is that in the United States we can't even agree on what the enchanted age should be. There is one age for getting a driver's license, another for being allowed to join military service and vote, and still another for doing all the things a minor cannot do. If that isn't confusing enough, some of those ages even vary from state to state.

Another more important reason is that our society is quite a bit more complicated than that of the bug-swallowing Bemba girls. Your teenage counterparts in Africa have only one set of directions to follow and very few temptations. (There is no conflict over whether to drink at the senior prom, for example, because chances are there is no senior prom and no firewater to begin with!) You, on the other hand, have to make hundreds of decisions about your life while you are dodging everything from cocaine to the urge to cheat on the biology final. Everyone, Newark to San Diego, makes those choices and handles those pressures in a different way; there is no head honcho or witch doctor to hand down hard and fast instructions. We as Christians do have an advantage there, because we have the Bible to follow. We will discuss that in detail later. As we know only too well, not everyone in the United States agrees. So as a result of all those differences, we end up with a very complex culture where we run around wondering what maturity even is, much less when and how it should come together.

That is the way it is. In our society, we are stuck with a life in which leaving the nest is a long process of trial and error. Unfortunately, because of all the questioning and confusion, it can be painful. Not necessarily physically (no whips and knives, hopefully) but emotionally where the hurt can be greater and last longer. Some teenagers do get through it without too much agony. Others don't.

Ice Wasson was one who didn't. A look at his method of dealing with leaving pangs shows why.

Ice was the kind of guy who made teachers cringe when he sauntered into their classrooms on the first day of school. They had a way of knowing that the "Cheap Trick" T-shirt and the tough mouth meant a semester full of wise cracks and assorted expletives. It did not take long to guess where he got the name Ice. Every feature on his face was as hard and cold as his attitude. In his cool way he kept himself from getting too close to anybody, and yet he called a lot of the shots for the rest of the kids. Most of those included cutting classes, losing the afternoons and evenings in a fog of drugs or alcohol, and defacing any piece of property that looked a little too neat and tidy for his taste. If Ice wanted to be famous, he had succeeded; his face was engraved on the memory of every policeman and school official in town. It was hard to miss the defiance he displayed in everything he did or didn't do.

Very few people saw something else Ice carried around with him, though. If you did manage to get close enough, you could see terror in his eyes. You would have never guessed it from fifty paces, but he was scared to death of what life was going to be like for a guy like him. He was hurting a hurt he could not really understand, so he covered up by lashing out at every established value he smacked into. It was strange how everyone was afraid of a guy who was really only afraid of himself.

Then there was Melanie Griffin. She found the process of leaving to be pretty heavy, too, but in a different way. Trouble is, nobody knew it. As a matter of fact, nobody even knew her. Melanie was a type that appears in every high-school classroom, the type whose picture nobody looks at when the yearbooks come out. Melanie was a shapeless girl: vague figure, baggy clothes, nondescript personality. Her face might have had some life, but it was difficult to get a glimpse of it. She sat in the corner of the room, back always against the wall, hiding behind a grim curtain of hair. Sometimes she did the assignments in school, sometimes she didn't. If they involved oral or group work, she immediately buried her face in her arms and pretended to sleep. But teachers never called her parents or referred her to counselors. For the most part they did not even know she was there, and that seemed to be exactly what she wanted.

Hard as it may be to see the similarities between them, Ice and Melanie were very much alike. Both of them were complex people tangled up in painful problems that probably began when they were just children. The types of behavior they exhibited as teenagers—the wild rebellion and the sullen withdrawal—were symptoms of the same thing: their struggle to leave and their fearful desire to stay at the same time.

Most of us, fortunately, did not grow up with the strikes against us that Ice and Melanie had to deal with. However, all of us have to face the prospect of leaving; and all of us have hang-ups, large or small, that could send the whole process shooting off in the wrong direction.

Think about yourself. Some of the people reading this book right now are like Ice in a way, perhaps minus the pack of cigarettes or the colorful vocabulary. Ice-types tend to lash out when the confusion seeps in and the going gets rough. Others are more like Melanie. The easy way out for them is to pull back and get numb. Still others react in different ways. In fact, there are probably as many ways to resist admitting to mixed-up feelings as there are people. In another chapter, we'll give you a chance to take a good look in the mirror and find out where you fall on the scale.

For now, though, the important thing to point out is that

those negative reactions do not solve anything, and they definitely do not produce leaving. At nineteen, Ice Wasson is doing time in a state penitentiary for armed robbery. He spits at the guards and threatens other inmates for dope. He is still striking out. Melanie, however, decided to hide from the world permanently. She committed suicide at seventeen.

Those who read this book will more than likely avoid arrest and a self-imposed death. But the same feelings that caused Ice and Melanie to destroy their lives can cause even the less extreme teenager to fall into one or more of a thousand different traps before the process of leaving is completed.

That is where the "adolescent problems" come in. You've probably heard of some of them until you're blue between the temples: teenagers and drug addiction, their drinking problems, the surge of failure and truancy in school, vandalism, teenage pregnancy and venereal disease—both products of increased sexual activity among young people.

Those problems and more bombard you from all sides. They have newspaper-reading citizens shaking their heads in disgust, and they have the people who care about you working very hard trying to find solutions.

Why do some teenagers drink, smoke, shoot up, and drag race down the freeway? Because they're showing the confused and crazy symptoms of something that, if it were understood, could be a very normal process instead.

Certainly we, the authors of this book, are not patting you on the head and saying, "Hey, go ahead and live a wild and crazy existence. You're just young and confused. You'll grow out of it." Actually, we look on you as almost-adults who need to learn how to avoid or deal with these major traps, and the minor ones, too, instead of being "pardoned" because you are just a child.

The minor traps are subtle ones on the inside that can quickly snag the unsuspecting teen. In their own way, they are as dangerous to the leaving process as a bottle of vodka or a can of white spray paint and a blank wall on a dark night.

There is the trap of never questioning anyone, but always doing the "right" thing and making decisions solely so as not to rock the boat. Then there is taking the low profile approach. That means never failing but never making a big splash with anything either. In that trap, just barely scraping by is the key.

Other pitfalls include an intense need to follow the crowd, a driving obsession with being the best at everything, a smothering tendency to hide in the library and graduate as a very unhappy valedictorian.

None of these traps, if you fell into them, would necessarily get you labeled as a "problem" teenager. But all of them could interrupt your leaving process and instead make you a very unsatisfied person still stuck in the protective custody of home long after you should be gone.

So a number of pits—some openly awesome and some sneakily camouflaged—yawn open at you, a person struggling with the need to break away. How do you leave completely and avoid falling into any of the traps? If you are in already, how do you get out?

The answering of those questions is what this book is really about. True, we hope to touch on both kinds of traps that can get a teenager off beat. That in itself though is not enough. Simply warning you about what is wrong and what is right won't necessarily keep you scarless.

What we want to do is show why a teenager goes into those yawning holes, sometimes with eyes wide open to the consequences. In our society (the one without the chicken-smothering ceremonies) we are left in the end to think things through and figure them out for ourselves. Tough as it is sometimes to do that, the outcome can be a lot more satisfying than knowing you sat on a chicken or that you have a permanent skull and crossbones etched on your left leg. As long as you are armed with some strong convictions and a good head full of information, you can create your own rite of passage. It won't be a purely physical one, but something powerful that takes place inside—so powerful, in fact, that it will untangle you from the ties of being a kid and escort you into your new world and your new self. As a matter of fact, that is where we have it all over the kids who get their manhood by way of ordeals in the jungle: ours continues inside as we keep on growing all our lives.

In this book we would like to explain some things and let you take it from there. No lectures. No shoulds. No no-no's. Instead, we will present the three major areas of your life for you to take a look at, things that need to be clear and strong before you can leave home emotionally and know you are going to make it. One area is the way you see yourself. Do you really know who you are? Do you like who you are? Can you deal with who you are?

The second involves the things outside yourself that you look to to help you make decisions. After all, we don't live in little plastic capsules where we touch nothing, and nothing touches us. We all have measuring sticks. What are yours? If there are none, or if they are the wrong ones, you could be in for complications.

The third is the way you communicate with other people, especially your parents. Are you an Ice who lashes out? Are you a Melanie who rolls up in a cocoon? Or are you somewhere in between on the wide spectrum of other possibilities?

Those three areas are difficult ones, but once they are squared away, you become like a good rock band. There's a beat and a style that's all your own. You do not try to be the Bee Gees if you are Styx. Instead, you live with a combination of sounds that are in harmony, on key, and up to tempo. You've got it together. You are ready to go on tour.

Helping you, the reader, get to that point is what we, the authors, are about. The method is simple.

For each of the three areas we will deal with here, we are going to present the stories of real teenagers, kids who lost the sound somewhere along the line. Hopefully, their stories will mirror some of the thoughts and feelings you are having, if not your actual experiences.

At this point, we hope to get every reader up and scrambling around for pencil and paper to take the self survey that appears in each chapter. It will give you a chance to apply what you read about other kids to yourself, in your own circumstances.

Next we will go back and explain why—why those young people we use as examples got themselves tied into knots. Knowing why is absolutely essential. Getting your own act together is like the rock group looking for a good combination. Those guys with the guitars and drums don't just jam until they stumble on something. They have to know exactly what they are doing. So do you.

Finally, we will present some alternatives. Not do's and don'ts, rights and wrongs, yes's and no's. Anyone old enough to read this book is past that. Instead, we will turn to the one sure resource that can keep things in perspective. The Bible is here, with God's image of this whole thing coming right at you. After all, that's where the original instructions to carry out this process came from. He is the one who said, "Kids, get off your duffs and start becoming somebody in your own right." He didn't use those exact words, of course. His, in Genesis 2:24, were more like this: "Therefore shall a man leave his father and his mother. . . ."

Notice he doesn't say, "Mothers and fathers, let go of your sons and daughters and let them do their own thing." He gives the job to you, the young person. He offers his everpresent help, but it is up to you to take it and run with it.

Just to prove that these alternative ways of dealing with things can work, we are also going to show how our real-life problem people used them and got on with the business of leaving in a productive manner. That way, no one has to simply take our word for it. By then, maybe some things will start to come together for you. We hope so.

Let's start with that self survey you took to decide

whether you're showing any of the signs of "leaving" yet. Here's how to score and see how you stand.

Take a look at your total. If you scored between 14 and 35, the fur is flying at your house! You are so anxious to break loose, and your parents are so frightened, that conflicts are probably occurring every day. You are fighting for freedom and most likely losing the battle. What we have to say here could help you.

If you fall in the 36 to 49 group, congratulations! You are what is called an "average adolescent." Sound boring? It isn't, really. You are having your twinges of the leaving bug, but there is a little interaction at home that is helping you to work it out pretty well. However, some understanding of what is happening can make the painful parts that may be ahead a little less so. Read on.

With a score of 50 to 70, it is safe to say that your parents are still enjoying being parents, and you are still enjoying the more protected, safe side of adolescence. This doesn't mean you are retarded! Leaving will come—and when it does, stand by. What you will read in this book should help prepare you.

Whatever stage of leaving you are in, you are not alone. Let's meet two other people who stumbled on the conflicts that can come when it is time to start breaking loose.

2

Who Do You Think You Are?

Bonnie was seventeen, blonde, and willowy. Unfortunately, those were not the things people remembered about her. If they noticed her at all, they recalled that she was very quiet and shy and couldn't look a person in the eye when she spoke. She was a loner with no real friends.

Teachers would remember she made excellent grades almost without trying, a fact that would make the average struggling student green with envy. But to Bonnie, that was no big deal. Making good grades didn't win her any attention or popularity from the other kids her age, and besides, it was just something her parents expected of her, something she did without question.

As the oldest of five children, Bonnie was responsible for going straight home from school every afternoon to look after her younger brothers and sisters while her mother went off to an evening job. She prepared dinner for her father and the children and also took care of an invalid grandmother who lived with the family. The list of duties was long, but Bonnie accepted it all without question. Even on Friday nights when her parents would decide to have a night out and go bowling or see a movie, Bonnie would stay home without complaint. By the time she was a senior in high school, their requests began to irritate her, and she secretly resented the burden. But each time, she was quick to assure her mother that she would be happy to do it.

Bonnie always did the "right" thing and lived up to the expectations set for her by her parents. She did as she was told, never talked back, and constantly looked for their approval. Yet for all of her teenage years, she had been a bored, lonely, unhappy person. At seventeen, she added confusion and fear to that miserable string.

A bachelor moved into the house next door that year. After meeting Bonnie and seeing how efficiently she ran her own home when her parents were gone, Tom offered her a weekend job cleaning his house and generally getting things organized for the week. She snatched up the opportunity eagerly and went to work the following Saturday. Tom watched her closely and was pleased.

Bonnie gave all of her attention to the job at hand and was not especially attracted to Tom. That's why even she was baffled when she accepted his suggestion of a physical relationship between them. Thus began a liaison that was to last several months. Whenever Bonnie went to work next door, Tom would approach her. Each time, she would agree to continue their affair.

Tom was thirty-five. It is really quite common for seventeen-year-olds to fancy themselves in love with older men. If a girl doesn't develop a crush on at least one handsome male teacher before she graduates from high school, she is very unusual! But for Bonnie it was nothing like that. She had never been physically drawn to Tom in the first place, and her encounters with him weren't pleasurable. She always felt very tense and awkward and wished she were anywhere else, doing anything other than what she was doing.

Most of that, of course, was because she hated what she was doing. It went against every value she had been taught, and it was totally out of character for her. She was also frightened that her parents would find out, for their disapproval was something she couldn't stand to think about. Yet she continued to carry on the relationship, and as she did, the self-accusing questions burned in her mind.

Why in the world was she doing something that was against her convictions, especially when it was bringing her absolutely no satisfaction? Did she have some kind of abnormal drive that was overcoming her will power? The questions wouldn't leave her alone. By the time she sought counseling, she was tied up in a tight, unhappy knot.

Lyle, at sixteen, was very different from Bonnie. People did notice Lyle because his appearance made him stand out in a crowd. He was 6'5", very thin, and he sported an unruly mop of curls that only drew attention to his large lips and bad complexion. However, it was more the frightened, wary expression he wore that drew amused glances from passers-by. Lyle always looked as if he expected people to lash out and cut him down.

There was good reason for that. He came from a broken home and lived with his mother. Dad lived in another town and was not around much; but when he was, he left Lyle with lasting scars. Although Lyle's father never physically hurt him, he cut him verbally even in public with scathing remarks about Lyle being slow and stupid.

School was indeed a struggle for Lyle. He was a slow learner, which was obvious from the labored way he spoke and moved his head to make a point, yet he was far from stupid. But Lyle's father was constantly irritated with him and never failed to embarrass him in front of other people. Lyle loved and admired the man in spite of that; at the same time, he was afraid of him. Lyle came away from each visit with a lower opinion of himself than he had had when he arrived.

Lyle wanted to do well in school, for his own satisfaction as well as his father's. But whenever a difficult assignment came up, he became a bag of jangled nerves. He was so afraid he wouldn't be able to handle the task, he just wouldn't try at all. Yet knowing he was not even giving the thing a chance made him uptight, too. No matter which way he turned, he met only frustration.

Like Bonnie, he was a loner at school. He had had one very close friend on whom he was completely dependent, but when the friend moved away, Lyle felt lost and was unable to forget that relationship and begin another one. He wanted very much to be like other people his age, but he seemed to go at it in the wrong way.

In the spring of his junior year, for example, he decided to go out for a track event and selected discus throwing. He had the size and power for it, but the discus requires finesse and coordination, two things Lyle was sadly lacking. After tangling himself up like a pretzel for several weeks, Lyle quit and felt even more defeated than ever.

He lapsed into a bleak depression, spending hours in his room alone doing nothing. Occasionally, at some minor provocation from his mother, he would become very angry, yell at her, and storm out of the house. After driving around town for hours he would return and say nothing about his furious exit. Then the cycle of withdrawal would begin all over again, and no wonder. He was failing academically, athletically, socially. Even his parents seemed disappointed in him. All of that certainly justified his depression. His mother finally became concerned enough to arrange for professional counseling.

Both of these stories are sad. Why are we telling them to you? We have two reasons.

The first is that all of us have problems, hang-ups, loose screws—call them what you will. But we tend to think, especially when we are in the very pits, that everyone else has their act together and we are the only ones thrashing around. We have introduced you to Bonnie and Lyle to show you that even quiet, low-profile types have their secret agonies. You may not have the same problems they have, but you can rest assured that you are not alone in the problems that trouble you. These are just two people we picked out of the flock to show that we all have hurts. Somehow, that can make a person feel better.

The second and more important reason is that Bonnie and Lyle have something very much in common. Although they showed it in different ways, they both suffered from what is called a NEGATIVE SELF-CONCEPT. The term itself isn't important, but an understanding of it is.

Your SELF-CONCEPT is the way you view yourself. It is the song you know is played just for you. It is what you see when you look in the mirror, what you hear when you listen to yourself talk, what you think of yourself in various situations. What kind of a student do you consider yourself to be? How do you feel you fit in at parties? What do you imagine other people think of you when they see you in the halls or work with you on a group project? The answers to those questions make up your self-concept. In a few minutes, we will give you a chance to test it out, but let's look at some more definitions first.

You may not realize it, but it is your self-concept that determines how you act, rather than the other way around. It isn't what you do, say, and look like that decides what you think of yourself. It is what you think of you that establishes the beat. That, in turn, can affect how other people respond to you—whether they catch your rhythm or walk away. Let's see how that works.

If you have a POSITIVE SELF-CONCEPT, you think good things about you. You see yourself as attractive or talented or fun to be around, so you act that way. Without appearing to be conceited, you attract members of the opposite sex, get attention, and have dates. You have the confidence to play the piano at a party or enter one of your paintings in a contest, and as a result gain a lot of satisfaction. You have friends and an active social life. You enjoy living.

On the other hand, if your self-concept is negative, you don't think much of yourself. If you met you in a crowd, you wouldn't want to be best friends. With a negative self-concept, you might be like Bonnie. She saw herself as dull, unattractive, and unimportant. She was bored with herself, so she assumed everyone else was, too. As a result, she stayed out of things and just played by the rules. People sized her up, thought she wanted to be left alone, and walked away. Because they did, she figured she must have been right about herself. There were many reasons for her feelings which we will get to later, but the point is that she thought she was "blah" so she acted "blah." Miss Blah was very much alone.

The same was true for Lyle. Again for a number of causes we will go into later, he thought he was stupid, slow, and clumsy. He shrugged his shoulders in defeat and went on his way. Naturally, after seeing the way he carried himself, everyone else agreed that, yes, Lyle was pretty much a klutz; and being treated that way only confirmed what he already thought.

Let's turn this idea inside out and look at it. Imagine that you have just walked into a room full of people you have never met before. Maybe it is the first day of class in a new school or a party at the home of a friend who lives in another town. Right away you notice four people.

Person One is cowering in the corner with her hair pulled over her eyes, glancing suspiciously at the group now and then but basically keeping her face turned away and looking as if she wants to be left alone.

Person Two is wearing a shirt that is almost as loud as his mouth. He's tearing around the room laughing like an idiot and bursting in on every conversation.

Person Three is standing in the middle of the room, but no one is talking to her. She is looking very openly at everyone and is obviously amused in a superior sort of way. Through it all she remains aloof.

Then there is Person Four. He is deeply interested in a discussion he is having with two other people. He listens to them, but he adds to the conversation, too. He smiles a lot and looks as if he is having a great time. So do the people with him.

Forgetting for a moment all you have been taught about being kind, loving, and considerate, think about which of those four people you would really want to get acquainted with right away. If you let your natural inclinations guide you, you would probably choose Person Four. He is open, friendly, happy. You want to be with him. And the reason? Because he feels good in that crowd. He is comfortable with himself, so everyone else feels at ease with him, too. He senses that and gains even more self-confidence.

What about the rest of them? Person One doesn't think she is worth being with. She gives off those signals, so you would just as soon not sit with her.

Person Two thinks he has to be a clown to get attention. He acts like one, and you are turned off. Fun is fun, but really!

Person Three thinks she is different from everyone else there. She acts "different," and you are put off by that.

If you took the time to get to know One, Two, and Three, you would find something attractive in each one. But you would have a hard time doing that, because they would refuse to believe it themselves. If you are like most of us, you would give up before long and leave One, Two, and Three to be the lonely people they were to begin with.

Now how about you? You may be a generally out-of-tune person, or you might just have a few bad sounds that blare out under certain circumstances. Any or all of that could be caused by your feelings about yourself. The first step in solving those problems is to find out just what your self-concept is. We have designed a survey here to help you do that. Grab a pencil and get set to take a good hard look at who you think you are.

SELF-SURVEY 2

Who Do You Think You Are?

Below you will find some statements to think about in terms of you. Read each one once and then write down your first impulse from the ratings given below. Don't dwell on any one question and don't go back and change any answers. Your first response will be the most accurate. Add the ratings for a total at the end.

> 1 always applies
> 2 often applies
> 3 sometimes applies
> 4 rarely applies
> 5 never applies

_____ a. It is easy for me to make friends.

_____ b. I try new things without hesitation.

_____ c. I see myself as physically attractive.

_____ d. I can say no to people without worrying that they will be hurt or that they will reject me.

_____ e. I see myself as gifted in some area (athletics or music or art).

_____ f. I am satisfied with the number of friends I have.

_____ g. I am relaxed when I walk into a situation where there are a lot of strangers.

_____ h. I think my parents like me.

_____ i. I am an above average student.

_____ j. When I meet someone new, they seem interested in me.

_____ k. I think God likes teenagers.

_____ l. I would rather do it than daydream about it.

_____ Total

If you have totaled up your ratings, you are ready to score. Let's see what your image of yourself is.

If your score is between 12 and 30, you think you are a winner, and you probably are! There is nothing conceited about it (unless you tell people how great you are hourly). You are lucky. You have a very positive self-concept. Many of the problems of "leaving" will probably pass you by. (But don't get a big head. You still need to know what you are up against.)

If you fall into the 31 to 42 group, you think you are "just average." You aren't real excited about you, and you definitely don't think anyone else is either. Your self-concept is more negative than positive, but it shouldn't be too hard to get you thinking good thoughts about yourself.

With a score of 43 to 60, you think you are a loser. You like yourself less than anyone you know. As if you didn't know it already, you have a negative self-concept, Pal. That can be changed, and it should be before you try cutting the apron strings completely.

You may not be pleased with the results of the survey, or you may be saying to yourself, "Yep, that's who I thought I was all right—a bore, (or an obnoxious nerd, or an intellectual oddball)." If that's true, it means your self-concept is a negative one. It also means your self-concept is wrong.

You can be wrong about yourself. Even though you've been eating, sleeping, and going to school with you for years, you don't necessarily know the *true* you. You've been looking at that face in the mirror every day since you were big enough to drag a chair up to the bathroom sink, but you haven't automatically been seeing what's really there.

Bonnie is a prime example of this business of mistaken self-identity. She saw herself as totally unexciting, with nothing going for her except her ability to make good grades. But Bonnie was lovely. With a little instruction in how to dress and take care of herself, and a little self-confidence glowing in her face, she could have been one of the most attractive girls in the senior class. Her natural intelligence, the way she could grasp things and make them clear, gave her a lot to say and enabled her to say it in a way no one else could. She was also a talented writer. If she had been a staff writer on the school paper or the yearbook, she could have made a number of friends and perhaps gained some recognition for herself. Even the compassion she was able to show for her disabled grandmother was special. That's a quality most people look for in a friend. If she had seen all of that, she would have been anything but lifeless and dull. Unfortunately, she was too far out of touch with herself to realize it.

Lyle, too, had his positive traits. He was a fine singer and had the potential to be a good musician. That isn't the "Mama's Little Boy" thing it was back when Junior couldn't play baseball because he was practicing his violin. Lyle's high school had an active choral department full of lively, fun-loving kids. Their director was constantly on the look-out for good voices, especially males. There was a world of fulfillment waiting there for Lyle, particularly because he was naturally eager to please and would work hard at something he knew he could succeed in. Hard as it may be to imagine, Lyle was not very far from being handsome, either. Without the wild hair-do and the frightened-rabbit look in his eyes, he would have been very attractive to some of the girls. A lot of women like a tall, slender man! Again, if only he could have seen those things in himself, his life would have changed.

You may be asking yourself, if Bonnie and Lyle had so much going for them, how could they have missed it? How could they not have seen those marvelous traits that made them so special? For that matter, where did their negative feelings about themselves come from in the first place?

Self-concept is not something that just happens for no reason, like a wart on your toe. It is the result, usually, of an entire childhood of being told and shown that you are a certain type of person. That comes most often from parents and is reinforced by brothers and sisters, teachers, and other kids in the neighborhood. When you are little, all of those forces together are a lot more powerful than you are, so you just accept what they are telling you. By the time you are a teenager and want to bust loose and be your own person, you can feel a little stuck with the image you already have. It is that stuck feeling that gets you into trouble.

All her life, Bonnie had gotten the message that if she just followed the rules and did what was right, she would be fine. It didn't matter whether she was having fun or finding any sparkle in living, as long as she never said no and never brought about any disapproval. By the time she became a teenager, she was convinced that she was a dutiful, respectful, but awfully boring person.

At seventeen, she was more than ready to break away a little and start making some choices on her own. Just living up to other people's expectations and getting a pat on the head wasn't enough anymore. But if she was just a rule-follower, how could she make independent decisions? How could she choose among alternatives if there was no adult around to point out which one was right? It really is not surprising that she was unable to say no to Tom. He was much older than she, and he was telling her that what he wanted was okay. Her image of herself as a girl who respects her elders wouldn't let her say, "Thanks, but no thanks." Yet when it was over, she turned around and plowed into another wall—what her parents would have told her was right. She was in what she saw as a hopeless trap.

Lyle's negative self-concept came about as the result of his upbringing, too. True, he was born with certain learning disabilities, but everyone has his handicaps. Mel Tillis stutters and Stevie Wonder is blind, but that hasn't kept them from being enormously successful. They obviously have a great deal of confidence in themselves. Lyle could have been happy, too, despite his natural slowness, had it not been for his father's constant criticism and public put-downs. From the time he was a little boy, he was told he was stupid and verging on spastic, so at sixteen he was convinced so much so that he was blinded to all of his good qualities. Lyle was like many parents when they look at a son's or daughter's report card. Their eyes slide over the A's and B's and zero right in on the D or F. He had concentrated for so long on his faults, they were all he could see in himself.

Lyle thought the only way to be happy was to improve where he was lacking. But his brief, embarrassing try at discus throwing only proved to him that he was the failure his father had told him he was all along. The only answer then was to give up and withdraw. Yet he was breaking loose a little, too, as was natural for his age, and sometimes he became angry thinking about how much he wanted to be different from what his parents thought he was. That's when he would fly from his room in a rage, hurl insults at his mother, and stomp out of the house. Just blowing off steam didn't work, though, and the depression would start all over.

WARNING! Our explanation of the reasons behind Lyle's and Bonnie's unhappiness is just that, an explanation. It should lead you to wonder why you feel as you do about yourself. Who knows? That may free you to look for your more positive side. But it shouldn't spur you to jump up and confront your parents with the mess they've made of your life! In the first place, it is safe to say your parents love you and have done their very best in raising you. As you may see for yourself someday, it is the toughest job going. Besides, since you started kindergarten and have been out of the house more waking hours than you've been in it, there have been thousands of other reinforcers besides your parents. It isn't a matter of blaming. It's a matter of understanding.

The real point is that you are now on the brink of adulthood. You are pulling away from the old ties, and in doing so you are taking responsibility for yourself. At the risk of seeming a little extreme, let's use the criminal as an example. He may be a compulsive thief and murderer because of the way he was brought up, but he's the one who has to go to prison when he's caught, not his mother and father!

So there you are with a self-concept that could be limiting your potential to be happy and fulfilled. It is up to you to do something about it. What can you do?

Again, you can start by realizing that any negative self-concept is a distorted self-concept. Look at Bonnie and Lyle. Who they thought they were and who they really were turned out to be completely different. If your self survey showed that you have a low opinion of yourself, you are wrong, too.

Of course, Bonnie and Lyle are only two examples. How can we get away with saying that everyone who has a negative self-concept is wrong about him/herself? If parents, teachers, the other kids on the bus are all telling you that you have nothing to offer physically, academically, athletically, musically, or socially, how can you be sure they aren't right?

For the answer to that we can turn to the Scripture.

To follow what we are saying here, your best bet is to pull out your own Bible (dust it off, if necessary!) and read for yourself, in context, the verses we mention. Let them ring some chimes in your head. Everyone will find something different that applies to him or her, and yet it will all be true. Let's try it.

Take a look at Romans 3:23. In this letter, the apostle Paul says to the people, "For all have sinned, and come short of the glory of God." That phrase "come short" is probably a familiar one to those who fell into the negative self-concept group on the survey. If you feel crummy about yourself, you have more than likely compared yourself to other people you admire and found yourself not quite up to par. You are not as smart as Joe Physics, or as adorable as Susie Smiley, or as All-American as Jack the Left Back. As a matter of fact, you just don't seem to be as good as everyone else at anything! That is pretty depressing.

But notice the verse says all have sinned and all have

come short. Not just you, but the valedictorian and the homecoming queen and the captain of the football team. When it comes to living here on earth and making choices, we all come up short. It is a state that leaves everyone in the dregs. None of us is as good as God, so in a way, we are all the same.

One thing you can do to raise your self-concept, then, is to stop comparing yourself to everyone else. Who you are is not determined by the looks and talents of the girl at the next locker. It is determined by God, and that makes you special. We'll come back to that later.

This idea of coming short of the glory of God has to do with who we are when we are outside of God. Sin actually means separation from God, so when we do not see ourselves clearly and are really messing things up, we are far away from him, and we feel lousy about ourselves.

That all started when Adam and Eve blew it in the Garden of Eden. Flip back to Genesis 3:8–19. Here we get a vivid picture of the two of them seeing themselves in a new light and hating what they see. They even dive into the bushes to try to hide themselves from God. They created a huge gap between themselves and him, and in so doing started a chain of guilt and shame that none of us have been able to avoid since.

But although God was angry with Adam and Eve, tossed them out of the Garden on their ears, and cursed us all with pain and sorrow, he didn't close up shop and go elsewhere to create another world that might not foul up so royally. Instead, he sent his Son to save us from ourselves. One of the most famous and often quoted verses in the Bible, John 3:16, sums it up very well: "For God so loved the world that He gave His only begotten Son, that whosoever believeth in Him should not perish, but have everlasting life." He did not create us and then leave. We are so special to him, he made the greatest sacrifice possible to save us.

What that can mean to you is that in spite of all the messages you may be getting elsewhere—your dad says you are lazy, your mom says you are disrespectful, your report card says you are stupid, and your empty social calender says you are a bore—God says you are special. Since he put you here—breathed in your nostrils the breath of life and made you a living soul (Gen. 2:7)—you are precious. If you have never been called that before, roll it around in your mind a little and get used to it, like you do a new tune on the radio. You'll like it!

In putting us here, God makes all the ground rules, and self-concept is one of them. His law states that your image of yourself should coincide with his. He created you as a likeness of himself. Check out Genesis 1:26–27. It says there that you are created in his own image. You are an image of God! A little scary? It shouldn't be, because he wouldn't have made you if he didn't know you had value. He declares, when you become a person, that you are important and there are no other forces that can take that away.

In reality, that is. In your own mind, though, your sense of self-worth might have disappeared before you even knew it was there! Here's why.

We are faced with two separate systems that assign value to people. One of those is the world's system. Here, people and things which are rare or extraordinary are assigned the highest value. Why do you think gold and diamonds are so expensive? Because they are rare and unusually beautiful. The same is true for pro basketball players, super rock stars, Grammy-Award-winning songwriters. They have very rare skills, so they are highly paid for what they do. Like diamonds and gold, they are considered valuable. Everyone else is just "average." But that is the world's opinion.

In God's system, everyone has value. As far as he is concerned, each of us is important right from birth. Each of us is unique, and thus rare, and therefore valuable. Before, we called you precious; now we're saying you're valuable. Pretty neat, huh?

What that all means is that in the world's system, people spend an awful lot of energy trying to convince themselves and others that they have value. They are constantly worrying about achieving that worth, and then holding on to it. Even the pro basketball player gets anxious about growing older and losing his touch. the rock star always has an eye toward the top forty, worrying that his popularity is going to fade with the fickle nature of listeners. If you decide that the world's system is the right one, you are faced with a lifetime of struggle and anxiety.

With God's system, you start out with value that cannot be taken away from you. God puts you here in his own image, so that with the first wail you let out as a baby, you are important. Your ability to do something with your life and to be happy in your relationships with other people is greater than in the world's system, because you are free from worrying about whether or not you are really worth anything. You don't spend a lot of time trying to create your own worth because you already know it's there. Instead, you can use your resources of time and energy to try some things until you find your niche. Happy in the knowledge that you are somebody special, no matter what anyone else thinks, you make friends more easily and are more successful in the things you try.

Let's plug that into an example. Say there is a play coming up at school, a big production. The drama and music departments are combining efforts; it is going to be performed at the community center, and getting a part means going up against a lot of competition. You have never been in a play before. You aren't in the chorus or the band, and you haven't taken drama. But for some reason the whole idea appeals to you, and you would like to give it a try. You daydream a little about having your name in the program, maybe with a picture next to it. Already the applause is ringing in your ears, and you can almost hear kids you have never even met calling to you in the halls, inviting you to parties, wanting to get to know you. Maybe your English teacher will recommend you for a scholarship.

The possibilities are endless, and you find yourself thinking about it more and more.

But if you have decided that the world's system is the one that assigns you your value, your dream about a part in the play is going to turn into a nightmare. After all, just as the people who do make it get a lot of positive recognition, the ones who really blow it get the kind of recognition nobody wants. That's a pretty big risk, having people nudge each other when they see you and whisper about what a fool you made of yourself at the tryouts. The more you think about it, the more you decide you'd better not take a chance. It's safer to just buy a ticket and watch the whole thing from the back row.

On the other hand, if you know that God's system is really the one that determines a person's value, you will probably go for it. Maybe some hidden talent will emerge at the tryouts, and you will land a leading role, or maybe you'll land the last spot in the chorus line. Perhaps you'll turn out to be tone deaf and get laughed right out of the auditorium in the first cut. But you know your worth is not dependent on other people's views of you. Sure, if the other kids laugh it will be uncomfortable. We would all rather not be the butt of the joke of the week in the cafeteria. But once the laughter has died down and everyone finds somebody else to make fun of, you won't feel any differently about yourself. You will know that you are not worth less because you didn't get a part or because you did get a few jeers. One of two things will have happened, depending on the outcome of the tryouts. If you have gotten a part, or even a position backstage, you have discovered a talent you never knew was there and never would have if you hadn't given it a try. If you haven't made the cast list, or even the usher list, you will just know that the theater is not your thing, and you will look around for something else—but you won't think any less of yourself. You know the people choosing the cast or the on-lookers doing the chuckling don't assign your worth. God does.

So what do you do if you have a low self-concept? Know God and trust him. Believe that what he says is true, that you do have value. It will be tough because you've been oriented to the world's system. If you stick with that, you won't try new things that present threats. But if you go with God's system, you won't be afraid to try, and try, and try again until you find activities and people that fill up your life.

Just remember, you have to believe first. The results will follow. It is just like self-concept. It is not what you do, say, or look like that determines your self-concept. It is what you believe about yourself that decides how you act and come across to other people. Turn to John 14:27 and see if this verse doesn't convince you: "Peace I leave with you, my peace I give unto you: not as the world giveth, give I unto you. Let not your heart be troubled, neither let it be afraid."

To prove that accepting the value God gave you can make you happier and more together, let's go back to Lyle and Bonnie. Both of their stories, we are glad to say, have happy endings.

Bonnie was able to discover all those wonderful, shining secrets about herself. It was slow and painful for her, as it would be for anyone. It is difficult to change an impression you have had for seventeen years. It was even more frightening to test her new ideas out. For a while it seemed to her that it might be safer to remain the person she was already used to than to try on the new Bonnie and risk finding out she was only a dream.

Finally she began to take some chances. Starting with the one thing she was sure of, her writing ability, she submitted a few of her poems to the literary magazine the seniors were putting together to leave as part of their class heritage. The staff liked them and asked her to come to a meeting to help select some of the other pieces. The meeting was held on a Thursday afternoon, and on the spur of the moment, two of the other girls asked her to a party they were having the following night. She agreed to go, and she did, but the twenty-four hours in between were nervous ones. She knew she would have to operate on new territory, and she wasn't sure she knew how. Actually that first party was not a Cinderella success, but she loosened up enough to at least enjoy watching what was going on. Her appearance there and her work on the magazine made her a familiar face in a particular crowd, and in a very short time she was invited to get-togethers almost automatically. "Of course, we'll ask Bonnie," seemed to be the general feeling. It didn't happen overnight. She remained a little uptight for a while, but gradually she blossomed.

There were still two important things she had to take care of. The first was Tom. She reported for work one Saturday, only long enough to quit. Concentrating very hard on looking right into his eyes, she told him she thought it would be best if they didn't see each other again, under any circumstances. For an instant she waited for the world to end or for his disapproval to shatter her, but the instant passed, and she was still there in one piece.

Then there was her responsibility for her family's care in the evenings. Even with her new involvement at school two afternoons a week, she could manage to slide in the back door just as her mother was leaving for work. But she had only been lucky about the weekend nights. Sooner or later she knew her mother would expect her to be available on a Saturday night when she had plans herself.

She took stock of what her obligations at home really should be and then approached her parents. Calmly and intelligently she told them she would like to have at least three days' notice if they wanted her to be at home on a weekend night and asked if they thought that was fair. Again she anticipated the trembling of the earth or at least the sting of disappointment from her parents, but neither occurred. The discussion was brief and a little awkward because none of them was used to dealing with things that way. But it was agreed in the end that Bonnie would have that courtesy paid her, if she would also announce her own plans in advance. Slowly but steadily, Bonnie was working her way out of the trap and liking herself more with every step. It showed in the shimmer on her face.

Lyle's struggle was a tougher one, but he built a strong foundation of confidence before he came up against the biggest obstacle.

At midyear he took a risk in signing up for mixed chorus and found it was something he enjoyed. He soaked up the favorable comments he received from the director. In March a boy in the twelve-member ensemble, which was made up of the best singers, moved away, and Lyle was asked to take his place. His self-esteem took an immediate upward surge that showed in everything he did. He made some friends, and they convinced him to cut his frizzed hair. Between that and the happiness in his manner, he even looked better.

When the final project in his humanities class was announced in April, the old feelings of frustration began to seep in again. It was automatic for him to shrug his shoulders and give up before he started. But an idea began to take shape. Maybe he could do some research on the history of the kind of madrigal singing his group was doing and get them to demonstrate for the class. Knowing he was on comfortable territory, he started in. The kind of elation Lyle felt at actually pulling the thing off, finishing something, was a kind he had never felt before. Admittedly, the written report was loaded with grammatical errors, but the content and organization were really very good, and the live performance in the classroom was a hit with everyone. It was the first grading period all year that Lyle didn't have to worry about passing the class.

But then there was the matter of his father. During the time that Lyle was rediscovering himself, he was with his mother, who was delighted that he was even out of his room much less functioning normally and happily. Lyle hadn't had to contend with Dad's criticism yet. One night just before school was out, his father called and offered him a job for the summer, which meant going away and living with him. Lyle accepted immediately, but he was scared.

He wanted his father to be proud of him, to like and respect him. It was important to Lyle to move away from the type of relationship they had always had. It was particularly crucial to do that without losing the new respect Lyle had gained for himself. He took to his room again, but this time to think things through. Isn't telling a person he is stupid a pretty cruel thing to do, even if it is true, he asked himself? Did his father's behavior mean there was something wrong with Lyle, or was it his father's problem? Lyle wasn't sure, but he was determined to find out. When school was out, Lyle gathered his belongings and his courage and went to live with his father.

The job, building a golf course, was a difficult one, but Lyle made friends with the landscaper, an older man who discovered that Lyle had a good eye for plants and flowers. The man and his wife took him under their wing like an adopted son, and he found himself being showered with homemade cookies and motherly hugs. Yet nothing Lyle did pleased his father, even though he was doing the best he could. Dad berated him in front of the crew, cut him down on the drive to and from work, and sliced him with criticism at the supper table. Lyle decided not to let his resentment build up and one evening explained to his father that he was convinced he did not deserve the kind of treatment he was getting. He stammered a lot and regressed into his old elaborate head-moving, but he got it out. He was disappointed when his father became angry and threatened to "kick him out of the house," but he was not cowed. He did not retreat. The next day, Lyle asked his older friend if he and his wife would take him in as a boarder for the remainder of the summer if his father did force him to leave. With that to fall back on, he continued his job and his good feelings about himself. His father's attitude didn't change, but he became sullen and less verbal in his attacks. Lyle stayed there until the end of August, sorry that his father was unhappy, but pleased that he had been able to get through with his head high. He returned home eager to start his senior year.

Neither Bonnie nor Lyle could ever have made those strides if they had not first believed in the value assigned them by God and thus raised their images of themselves. With the positive self-concepts they now possess, they will eventually be able to leave completely and become successful, productive adults. They have discovered their own beat and a harmony that is pleasant to their own ears. They are ready for the big concert tour.

The same can be true for you. The realization that you were placed here already possessing value can free you to discover things about yourself you never knew existed. A change in your view of yourself will reverse the way you look and act—and the way most other people treat you. It will even relieve your anxieties about leaving and making it on your own. You will have a new tune in your heart—one that was written for you alone.

3

Measuring Sticks

Mark crouches at his desk in history class, gnawing at his fingernails and staring in agony at the test in front of him. He doesn't know a single answer. His mind is a blank. But that smart girl in the next row isn't keeping her paper covered, and passing the course hangs in the balance. . . .

Laurie hangs up the phone and stares glumly at the wall. Keith Martin, hunk of all hunks, has finally asked her out. But he wants to take her to an all-night beach party. Her parents, she knows, will never go for that. Of course there is always good old Kate, who would be willing to say Laurie had spent the night with her. . . .

Brenda tosses the list of course descriptions onto the floor and buries her head in her pillow. Her dad has laid down the law: nothing but college prep classes next year. But the school has added two commercial art courses, and art is really her first love. He would never know until it was too late to change. . . .

Those are only three examples of decisions teens are faced with every day. The list is endless. Yet if most adults knew what was on a teenager's mind, they would probably snort and say, "Ha! You think you have problems now? Just wait until you grow up!"

But right now, every one of those choices probably seems just short of life or death in significance. No matter how insignificant the decisions of adolescence may seem to someone who has left the teen years in the dust, those choices are tremendously important to the teen who is in there sweating them out.

Besides, some of the decisions teenagers come up against these days are "adult" problems. The choices a girl or guy makes about sex, drugs, alcohol, driving, school courses, and even friends, can shape that person's whole life— or possibly distort it. Also, the very act of making decisions can help prepare a teen for the years ahead, when choices—tough ones—will be hitting like snowfall against a windshield.

In the 1960s Alvin Toffler wrote a book, *Future Shock*. His predictions of what life was going to be like down the road a few years shook up society. Time has proven that Toffler was frighteningly close to the truth. He said that change was happening faster than ever before, so fast that parents then wouldn't be able to imagine the kinds of decisions their kids would be faced with as adults.

Some of those kids are you. Look at the issues you are going to have to deal with on an almost everyday basis. Issues involving computers, test-tube babies, nuclear power, space travel, movies and television where nothing is taboo, completely different roles for men and women. It could become mind-boggling if a person does not have a pretty good method for making decisions. It is vital to be able to select wisely from among all alternatives. But now the bottom-line question: how?

Well, as easy as decision-making may appear for some people, it very seldom is. It is as complex as a hit rock song: it sounds "together," but you wouldn't believe the pieces it takes to make it up or the time to get it just right. If we take decision-making apart and separate the process into its pieces, it might be easier for you to fit them all together.

First, it is helpful to understand that part (and notice we

say *part*) of what happens when you make a decision is that you make a VALUE JUDGMENT. That is, you make your choice by comparing two or more values and then choosing the one that means the most.

Let's say the crowd you run with wants to buy a six pack and head for the beach with it, just for fun, just to see what it's like. If you say sure, in spite of the fact that common sense, the law, and your complete dislike for the taste of beer all tell you not to, you probably value acceptance by the crowd above other things. If you say no thanks, you may feel it is important to obey the law or your parents or both!

Some set of values or "important things" means a great deal to you. That also determines in part how you make decisions. We call that your FRAME OF REFERENCE. In the pages ahead, we will also refer to it at times as your REFERENCE POINT. Whatever we call it, you might think of it as glasses you can look through to figure out where you are and where you want to go with that choice.

Here is another example that might help make this clear.

Have you ever moved to a new town and wondered how in the world you were going to find your way around without getting hopelessly lost? Chances are you picked out a familiar landmark and made your way to new places by using that as a reference point.

"You live on White Street?" you ask someone. "Where is that from the Hillside Mall?"

To you the whole town seems to be built around the Hillside Mall. If you can see it, you know you are headed in the right direction and you know which way to turn. You aren't wandering around hoping you will stumble on your destination. And if you can see it, you will always be able to find your way home.

The same thing is true in learning to play the piano. Where is that note from middle C, you will ask yourself.

Or learning to type. Where is that letter in relation to the home row?

In each of these situations, there is a reference point. If you keep that reference point in mind—be it middle C, the Empire State Building, or ASDFJKL;—everything else seems to fall into place.

Decision-making involves something similar. Without a frame of reference, the decider doesn't see things in any kind of logical way, and makes some "dumb" choices as a result.

One part of that frame of reference should be someone special—yourself! We devoted all of Chapter 2 to helping you get to know yourself, because that's as essential to your ability to make decisions as it is to your happiness. If you know the real you—in other words, if you have a positive self-concept—you also know what you want. Your set of values is pretty clear.

Okay, that's part of it. Self is a necessary reference point. But everyone needs an additional one to go along with that.

Simon and Garfunkel once recorded a sad, haunting song entitled, "I Am a Rock."

"I am a rock, I am an island . . ." they said. "I touch no one and no one touches me."

Unfortunately, some people do try such isolation. But that doesn't solve anything. It just complicates the decision-making process. Here is an example that drives the point home.

In the Army, basic trainees are put through night training so they can learn to maneuver in the dark. One of the exercises they do involves assembling everyone in a room which is pitch black. The instructor turns on a small light with a beam about as wide as a pencil and tells the recruits to follow its path with their eyes and remember exactly where it moves.

So thirty or forty people watch a light move—up, down, sideways. When the main lights are turned on, all forty of them report how the light moved around with no pattern.

Trouble is, the light did not move. It remained exactly where it was at the beginning of the exercise. But because they were unable to see other things in relation to the light, they had no frame of reference other than themselves. The movement of the light became distorted.

So, when you have no reference point outside of yourself, clear, accurate judgments cannot be made. It is actually pretty rare for a person to be quite that self-oriented. We all know, for instance, that it is against the law to pick up a candy bar in a store and walk out without paying for it, even if we would really like to have it. Hence, the majority of us don't shoplift. Unless something else is going on—we are starving to death, maybe—we are using the law as one frame of reference outside ourselves. Prisons bulging with inmates testify to the fact that there are other reference points.

However, we do occasionally find a person who uses mostly himself or herself as a frame of reference. Whatever feels good at the moment determines how the decision will be made. This guy or gal doesn't give much thought to what might happen down the line as a result of an action.

Stacey is this kind of person. Stacey had just turned sixteen when the real problems began, and it became obvious that she was operating under the "if it feels good, do it" philosophy.

Although she packs a little more weight than she probably should, Stacey is good-looking. She has large, soft brown eyes and thick shiny hair that shows she takes a lot of time with her appearance. The clothes, the make-up, the nail polish—everything about Stacey is right on.

She also lights up when she talks, flashing a dazzling smile and using her hands to help her out. Stacey does a lot of that to attract guys. She likes attention from boys, which is why she was so miserable at the private all-girl school she attended as a sophomore. Not only were there no males, but also there weren't any other girls who thought the way she did.

It was boring, so Stacey cut classes and strolled around in the mall instead. She never thought about how she was going to explain her absence the next day. The decision to skip school was based on today.

Eventually she got caught, and then there was no getting out of going to classes. She went, but she refused to do any work. There were no thoughts of, "If I don't do these assignments I'll fail and be a sophomore for the rest of my life." It just came down to the fact that school was dull today, so today she wasn't going to work. Naturally she came home with some pretty dead-looking report cards, and her mother grounded her. No dates. No parties. No guys. Ouch!

But Stacey got around that. She unlocked the screen on her bedroom window and sneaked out at night. Never mind how she was going to get back in. She'd worry about that later. All she knew was that she had to get out of the house. She was apprehended at that, too, by a policeman who picked her up for being out after curfew. The explanation from Stacey?

"Sorry, officer, but my mother kicked me out of the house, and I had no place to go."

With Stacey, it was always a matter of getting away from the heat of the moment; but that often meant jumping right from the grill rack into the charcoal. Most of her decisions were similar to cutting off your hand because your finger hurts; you're left without a hand, but at least your finger doesn't hurt anymore.

Don't be misled, though. Stacey isn't all "bad." She does have a conscience, and she really doesn't like to hurt people. It's just that *she* is her only frame of reference; she comes first. That's what happened in the incident with Jerry.

Stacey liked to have at least two guys on the string at all times, just to keep things interesting. About the time her sophomore year ended, she was seeing both Jerry and Alec.

Alec was very much like Stacey—basically self-centered and live-for-the-moment. Their relationship was at times disastrous, but his domineering way gave Stacey a sense of security, however false it might have been.

Jerry, on the other hand, was what they used to call in the old movies "a sweetheart of a guy." He was smaller than Stacey and very eager to please her, so she could boss him around very easily. He would grin his shy grin and give in to her demands and whims. He would have gulped down the nearest tsetse fly before he would ever intentionally hurt her.

Stacey knew all that. Still, the night she and Jerry went roller-skating and Alec appeared, Stacey panicked. Not two hours before, she had lied to Alec when he had asked her out, telling him she was grounded again and couldn't leave her room. That had been easier than admitting she was going to be with someone else. When Alec saw her with Jerry, he also saw red and started rolling up his sleeves.

Of course, a fist fight between the two guys would have been nothing short of a massacre, but Stacey wasn't worried about Jerry being broken into small pieces. She just couldn't stand the thought of a big scene or of losing Alec.

So Stacey walked smoothly up to Alec, took his arm, and told Jerry to get lost. The tense moment vanished, Jerry left in humiliation, and for the moment Stacey was on an even keel again. The next day she felt ashamed, so somehow she managed to win Jerry back. Until next time. . . .

We will fill you in later on what has happened to Stacey. Meanwhile, let's look at another kind of frame of reference. This one is the opposite extreme of the self-centered type. This person uses everyone else as a reference and never self. In a quiet, eager-to-please way, this person has almost as many problems.

Bret is a "pleaser." It is a little unusual for a guy to fall into this role, but it happens. We introduce you to Bret so you won't get the mistaken idea that it is only girls who try to please all the people all the time.

Like Stacey, Bret is no slouch in the looks department. He has clean, sharp features and a good build. Girls like his voice, which is kind of soft and husky. He definitely has a lot going for him.

But even at seventeen, with his voice completely changed and his bout with acne a thing of the past, Bret was totally unsure of himself. He could barely swallow without looking around to see if everyone else was swallowing, if his parents said it was okay to swallow, if the Bible sanctioned swallowing, and if he could get arrested for swallowing! He was certain he wasn't good enough and could never measure up to what other people expected, but he was sure going to try.

As a result, Bret always had to dress precisely in the style of the moment. It was almost as if he had a fear of being out of step with current fashion. If jeans were worn faded that year, he washed his new ones twelve times before he wore them. Had the fashion world suddenly decided to do away with ears, he would have hurriedly whacked his off.

Bret was so anxious to win approval from all sides, he constantly looked stiff and cautious, forever on guard. He wasn't happy. Who would be, trying constantly to be all things to all people?

He slaved until dawn some mornings over his homework in an attempt to make good grades to please his teachers and parents. Then he spent most of the day in school trying to keep up an air of cool indifference, because, of course, only nerds care about school.

Bret went to church because he didn't want to make waves with his parents. But although he went through all the motions on Sunday mornings, his mind would drift right out the stained glass window to whatever the rest of his friends were doing. He never admitted to any of the nonchurchgoers in his group that he ever darkened the door.

As a result of Bret's concern with avoiding conflict at all cost, his relationships with other people were a mess. He never argued with his parents, even on the rare occasions when they were, as all humans are from time to time, unreasonable. But the resentment would build up in him until every so often he would explode over something ridiculous and leave his folks with their mouths open.

The guys he hung around with tended to take advantage of him. Bret had a car his senior year and the word got around fast that he was willing to cart people back and forth to school, take carloads to basketball games, chauffeur to the pizza place afterwards, and even wait for hours in the car while his friends escorted their dates to their doors. There were times when Bret became annoyed with that setup, but did he say anything? Did he put his foot down and say, "No way"? Not at all. He just went around feeling used and abused and never doing a thing to gain control.

But Bret's relationship with his steady girlfriend, Laura, was the all-time worst. Where she was concerned, he couldn't seem to do anything right.

In the first place, Bret did not choose Laura. They just sort of ran into each other at a party, and because she seemed interested in him it was easy to stay with her. He hated gatherings where there were a bunch of people he didn't know, so she made the situation more comfortable.

After a while, Bret deceived himself into thinking he really was crazy about her. In reality he wanted a girl with some deeper interests than just gossip, cheerleading, and the color of her eyeshadow. But he let himself think she was satisfying his needs and ignored those deeper wishes.

Laura was the boss of the outfit. Bret's usual words to her were, "What do you think we should do?" and "Whatever you decide is okay with me."

Trouble is, the whole thing was doomed from the beginning in spite of his lack of backbone. When something did go well, he couldn't take the credit because it had been Laura's decision. When there were problems, he could always blame her. She'd get mad and they'd break up.

Bret was always secretly relieved when that happened. Yet, when Laura inevitably called and wanted to get back

together, he would make the decision to accept—not because he wanted to, but because Laura wanted to. Then the
whole cycle of pleasing and resenting would start all over.

That all came home to roost when the question of their
physical relationship came up. Bret really did not want to
sleep with Laura. He did not love her, and somewhere down
in the real self he had not bothered to get to know, he felt
that love and sex ought to go together somehow. Besides, in
spite of his current ill feelings about spending time in
church, he really did believe in what the Bible said about
premarital sex.

It would seem that his decision on the matter would be
clear cut. Not so. There were the other guys to consider.
Bret had been going with Laura long enough that if he
didn't have a war story in the locker room soon, he was in
definite danger of losing face.

Laura was pushing for it, too, almost as if it would prove
to her that Bret loved her or that she was as attractive as
she hoped she was. Bret didn't know what her reasons
were, but if it was what she wanted, he thought he had
better give in. If he didn't, he was sure their whole relationship would be over and he would feel like a failure, even
though he didn't care that much about her.

We will let you know later what happened to Bret and
Laura. Right now, let's take a closer look at you.

It is possible to have a little of Stacey, the self-centered
type, and a tad of Bret, the pleaser, in the same person. In
fact, every teenager who struggles in healthy ways to re-
solve the confusion that often rages inside will experience
some of both. At this point, it is important to know toward
which extreme you lean. To find that out, grab a pencil and
take this little survey.

SELF-SURVEY 3

What Is Your Frame of Reference?

Below you will find some statements to think about in terms of you. Read each one once and then write down your first reaction from the ratings given below. Don't spend too much time on any question and don't return to any to change your answers.

A word of caution: this quiz has a built-in lie detector. If you are not completely honest, it will show in the results (and your decision-making skills will self-destruct!).

Unlike the other quizzes, this one has two parts. Add the totals separately because the results will be interpreted separately.

    1   always applies
    2   often applies
    3   sometimes applies
    4   rarely applies
    5   never applies

Part 1

_____ a. People accuse me of being selfish.

_____ b. I make my moves without asking for advice.

_____ c. I hate it when people tell me what to do.

_____ d. I seem to turn people off.

_____ e. I am told I am loud, obnoxious, and rude.

_____ f. I have feelings but I don't know where they come from.

_____ g. I get into fights.

_____ h. Guilt is not something I feel a lot.

_____ i. I take advantage of people.

_____ j. I worry more about today than tomorrow.

_____ k. I am bossy.

_____ l. I am willing to lie to get out of trouble.

_____ m. I don't think people realize that sometimes I can feel hurt.

Part 2

_____ a. I feel guilty about my relationships with other people.

_____ b. I resent the other people in my life.

_____ c. I change my mind after I have decided something.

_____ d. I say yes when I would really like to say no.

_____ e. I feel like I am not quite good enough.

_____ f. I leave relationships feeling hurt.

_____ g. I feel like two different people.

_____ h. When a new situation comes up, I feel like running.

_____ i. I think people take advantage of me.

_____ j. I would rather avoid conflict than fight.

_____ k. I talk myself out of my hunches, intuitive feelings, first reactions.

_____ l. I ask people for advice.

_____ m. I have feelings (like anger or sadness), but I don't know where they come from.

_____ Total for Part 1

_____ Total for Part 2

If you were completely candid in taking the quiz, your totals should look something like this: (1) You scored 13 to 33 on Part 1 and 46 to 65 on Part 2; or (2) You scored 46 to 65 on Part 1 and 13 to 33 on Part 2; or (3) You scored 34 to 45 on both Part 1 and Part 2.

If you fall into category (1) above, that means you rarely consider anything outside yourself as a reference point. You are more like Stacey than Bret. No, you are not rotten to the backbone! You just need to read on!

If you find yourself in category (2) above, you consider everyone except yourself as a reference point most of the time. You are more like Bret than Stacey. No, you are not totally wishy-washy! You, too, just need to read on!

If you are in the (3) category above, you are well-balanced. You know and consider yourself in making decisions, but you consider outside sources as well.

If by chance you scored between 46 and 65 on both parts or between 13 and 33 on both parts, that does not compute! If you know you were not quite honest with your answers, take the quiz again. If you think you were, go back and review Chapter 2. Chances are, you don't quite know yourself well enough yet.

Knowing whether you tend to use yourself or everyone else who happens by as your frame of reference for decision-making, you can now take a serious look at the need to strike a balance between the two. It certainly is not healthy to use only yourself as a reference point. What happened to Stacey is evidence of that.

Just before she turned seventeen, Stacey discovered she was pregnant. Anxious to extinguish the anguish that was causing her, she had an abortion. But because she does have a conscience, she was then plagued by guilt. The best way to eliminate that was to marry, so she quit school and talked small, quiet Jerry into making her his wife. When married life became tough, cramped as they were into one room of Jerry's parents' house with next to no income, Stacey got nervous and restless. She felt things closing in on her, so she called Alec. They started to see each other secretly. The damage of that to her already weak marriage meant an early divorce. Within six months of the wedding, Stacey was out on her own, and she was still only seventeen.

Without job, education, or money, Stacey had no choice but to move back home. That was horrible. There were constant verbal, and at times physical, battles with her mother and sisters. Finally she got a job as a waitress and scraped up enough cash to get into a tiny apartment, with her mother's help on the cleaning deposit.

Her mother also made a down payment on a car for her, but Stacey chose to buy new clothes instead of making payments. She soon lost the car.

She also chose to sleep in several mornings instead of going to work. She soon lost her job.

Eventually, of course, she lost the apartment.

The comfort of the moment, whatever was easiest for Stacey, determined every choice—and got her nowhere.

Although Bret is Stacey's direct opposite, his way of making choices—that is, to try to do what he thinks everyone else wants—has taken him just as far off the track.

Just before graduation, Laura, too, became pregnant. Bret's parents thought he should marry her, so he did, giving up his plans to go to college. It seemed like the only thing to do to keep everyone happy. Everyone but himself, of course. He hated the thought of spending the rest of his life with Laura, but he did not say so.

He also hated his job as a "landscaper" for the city park system. He picked up trash, pulled weeds, mowed lawns, and resented every minute of it—but he said nothing.

As the months brought them closer to the baby's birth, Bret became more and more angry, but since he stowed all that frustration away, it festered inside. Then one day, he did something completely out of character. He came home to their dingy little apartment after shoveling snow all day to find that Laura had spent the rent money on an enormous Christmas tree and several boxes of expensive ornaments. Something snapped.

Bret tore the apartment apart, literally. He threw books, ripped magazines, and broke dishes. With pieces of furniture overturned and a lamp smashed to bits, he was through. Then he tossed some things into a bag and took off, leaving Laura in a corner trembling and confused.

She didn't see or hear from him for three months. By the time he was a few towns away he started to calm down, but he was so confused about his own feelings and so afraid to face the conflicts he had left behind, he just could not go back.

It ought to be clear by now that everyone needs to get the scales tipped evenly in decision-making: respecting self balancing out respecting others. It really is not as difficult as you might think. It involves just two steps.

Again, the first is what we talked about in Chapter 2:

know yourself. If you take the time to find out what you want, what is important to you, you form values. You can then use those values to make value judgments. For example, if becoming well-educated is important to you—it is one of your values—you will use that value to decide to go to geometry class every day instead of cutting out with the other kids to go to Burger King.

But wouldn't you know? Even making value judgments involves a few "catches."

Number one, attaching importance to your values doesn't happen in a vacuum. Other things are going on all the time. Suppose you have a geometry test tomorrow, and you desperately need to stay home and memorize theorems in order to pass it. But you get a phone call; your best friend's father just died; you are needed. Suddenly the values shift, and you are off to lend a shoulder and an ear. Most of the time in a decision, one value is pitted against another, so you have to choose between two points on your frame of reference. Complex, huh?

Number two, your value system is constantly changing as you and your circumstances change. Let's go back to the same example.

Education is important to you. You would never think of cutting geometry class to go to Burger King. But then one day you fall in love. Suddenly one guy (or girl) is the center of your world, and this center of your world checks out to the B. K. every afternoon. Since pleasing the love of your life has become your top priority, you might just take the chance and cut a time or two.

Or this could happen. You are so enthralled with your success in geometry that you decide to become a mathematician. Then your SAT scores come in and you find out you are in the lowest percentile in math. The world turns upside down, so does your frame of reference, and within two weeks you have transferred to a horticulture class.

Of course, you might also decide that what you want is stronger than what the tests tell you and take steps to change the situation: get a tutor, take remedial math courses, and retake the SAT for a better score.

The plot thickens, doesn't it?

Now for the second step. Be aware of who other people are and what they are asking of you in a decision situation.

Think back for a moment to when you were about twelve, just starting junior high. The kids your age (and possibly you) were often loud and obnoxious and even cruel to each other. Those were the days when a bunch of guys would gang up on one fella and toss him, half-dressed, out of the locker room into the hall. Or a group of giggling girls would paw through a friend's purse, find a secret love note she had never intended to send, and drop it on the unrequited lover's desk.

The reason is not that all twelve-year-olds are creeps. It is just that at that age the first urge to distinguish self from authority appears. All of a sudden there are choices that were never there before, and preadolescents want every-body to know they can make decisions alone, right or wrong! They are so busy doing that, there is really very little time to take other people's feelings into account.

But by the time a person is fourteen or fifteen, the fact that there are alternatives in every situation is old stuff. (In fact, there are times when it is almost a pain in the neck!) There is no need to run around drawing attention to it anymore. There is time to think about other people. It is time to strike a balance.

Here is how that delicate equation works. Let's say you are in a restaurant; it is a Saturday and you have dropped in to have a sandwich for lunch.

At one table there is a group of rowdies. They are loosen-ing the tops on the salt and pepper shakers, turning the water glasses upside down, and calling the waitress "babe." They stay for two hours, never order anything, and make snide remarks about the clothing, conversation, and facial features of everyone around them. Their frame of reference: themselves.

At a table for one is a sixteen-year-old girl who is taking a lunch break from the drugstore next door where she works. She only has an hour, but because of the "radical" crowd at the next table, thirty minutes slip by before the waitress comes to take her order. Still, she doesn't say anything because she doesn't want to impose. When she finally does order and gets her food, it is a B.L.T. She ordered a cheeseburger. She hates conflict, though, so she eats it and goes to the register to pay. The cashier gives her the wrong change, but because of the rude remarks about her bushy eyebrows coming from the wild table, she just wants to get out of there. She takes off with two dollars less in her pocket than she should have had. Her frame of reference: everyone but herself.

Then there is you. You are with friends. It is important to you right now to have a big roast beef sandwich and a cup of hot chocolate and talk. You want to have a good time. You wait patiently for the waitress, but after fifteen minutes of watching her being monopolized by the table of clowns, you politely tap her on the shoulder and ask if your party can order. You can laugh and joke with your friends, but no one from another booth turns and glares at you because you are causing a disturbance, because you aren't! When the waitress brings your order, it is a disaster. You let her know you understand that she is being hassled today, but you will find a socially acceptable way to get it straightened out. When one of the unruly kids remarks loudly that you have a nose like a hawk, you ignore it and he eventually gives up trying to get you riled. You get what you came for—a good time. Your frame of reference: a mature combination of knowledge of your own needs and consideration for others.

Just in case you are not quite sure this is all possible, dust off your Bible again. Have a look at Matthew 22:39. Here a sly lawyer asks Jesus which is the great commandment in the law. Jesus answers him in part by saying, "Thou shalt love thy neighbor as thyself."

Let's examine that closely. Jesus is commanding two things: one, love yourself, know who you are, care about you; two, love your neighbor, think about his feelings as much as you do your own. Do both, Jesus tells us.

That could be difficult. But one thing that might help you when doing both gets tough is to remember you are a teenager. (How could you forget, right?) It is written in your contract to feel the following: (1) unsure about exactly who you are; (2) like a different person every day (or even more often than that); (3) confused, scared, and excited about all of the above!

That goes with the territory of being a teenager. You are growing, learning, changing faster than you ever will again. With all that going on, it is okay to feel a little crazy.

The important thing is to accept that as part of who you are. If you think when you go to sleep at night that you are going to drop chemistry because it is too hard and then wake up the next morning with a perfectly balanced equation for the reaction of hydrogen and neon planted precisely in your brain—don't think you are losing your mind. Just weigh both sides carefully and then make your choice.

Accepting that little bit of madness in yourself can also help you understand the other people you will be considering while making decisions. Give your girlfriend or boyfriend a break. Let your date have a chance to be a little weird instead of tossing in the class ring (ID bracelet, football sweater, or other symbol of attachment) at the first sign of trouble.

Think about that the next time your sister snatches her blouse off your back when only the day before she opened her closet to you and generously told you to wear anything you wanted anytime!

And let's face it, those momentary lapses are not the exclusive possession of the teen world. Parents, teachers, professional quarterbacks, and lead guitarists are all human. You might try being tolerant of that when their off-the-wall reactions figure into your decisions.

So far we have talked only about yourself and those close to you as factors in your frame of reference. But naturally nothing in life is going to be quite that simple. There are two other measuring sticks to consider.

The first is what we call "society." It is the big picture—the law, morality, manners. As a frame of reference all by itself, it isn't the best. Right now society might be accepting a lot of things that just don't set right with you. Maybe you aren't into living together or drinking socially. But there are some things that society sets up which it is a good idea to follow.

One, obviously, is the law. It is not up to us to decide whether it is right to steal, kill, maim, embezzle, litter, or double park our cars. The law does that for us. It is better to use it as a reference point than to end up in the slammer.

Another is common courtesy. It is acceptable in society to say please and thank you and hold the door open for a lady carrying a set of infant twins and three bags of groceries. It is not acceptable to swear at the principal and put your feet on the desk in the classroom. Fitting into those standards makes you acceptable and gives you a certain amount of class.

So society is like a gauge for measuring outward behaviors. But what about the inside stuff, the part that motivates us to want what we want? That is where God comes in.

Flip in your Bible to Matthew 15, right around verse 8. The scribes and Pharisees have been giving Jesus a hard time because his disciples broke tradition and didn't wash their hands before eating. As always, he has an answer for them. He says this is just what Esaias prophesied about them, that, "This people draweth nigh unto me with their mouth and honoureth me with their lips; but their heart is far from me."

Sure, they say all the right things and go through the proper motions, but their motivation, the driving force inside them, is all out of whack. Man looks at outward appearances, but God looks to see how things are inside.

This motivation we are talking about is a basic measuring stick for our choices in life. Unlike society or our own priorities, it doesn't change. It is the one constant, driving force behind your knowledge of yourself and your consideration for others.

For example, both Bret and Stacey always look as if they just stepped out of *Seventeen* magazine, but their reasons for that are different. Stacey wants attention from guys. Bret doesn't want to be out of step.

Now look at Matthew 22:37–38. You'll find this: "Thou shalt love the Lord thy God with all thy heart, and with all thy soul, and with all thy mind. This is the first and great commandment."

There is your motivation. It happens when you let God love you as you are, no strings attached. Let God have a crack at you, let him be your motivation, and you will find a lot of things falling together.

A word of caution here, though. This works very closely with knowing yourself and being very honest about who you are. For an example, let's look back at Bret again.

He went to church purely because it was expected of him, but he never really enjoyed it. Half the time he found himself nodding off in the pew, and there were even Sundays when he faked the flu just so he wouldn't have to go. Yet he never admitted that to himself. He really thought he was doing the right thing.

There are a lot of people like Bret. There are also others who are a little less "acceptable" but a tad more honest.

Given the freedom to choose, these people decide church is not for them—not because it is boring or gets them out of bed too early, but because it makes no sense to them. They are aware enough of themselves to know that this particular church has no meaning for them. They are actually closer to the truth in their lives than people like Bret, because here is what can happen.

They don't like what that church is saying, so they look a little further. "What does God look like to me?" they ask themselves. How can I relate to him more meaningfully? These folks are in a position to find a place where they can come to know God. The Brets of the world, on the other hand, are just quick to say, "Hey, I go to church every Sunday, so get off my case!"

Now don't jump to the conclusion that we are discouraging you from going to church! We are encouraging you, though, to look at your motivation for going. If you are honest with yourself, God can speak to you and help that motivation to be an accurate measuring stick. If you are kidding yourself, there is no way God will come through.

Here is another example. You will notice that many of the problems both Bret and Stacey had involved their attitudes about sex. That is not unusual. Because of the biological changes that take place in the body during the teen years, it is natural to have the desire to be close to somebody physically. At the same time, because of the conflicting reports you get from parents, teachers, ministers, friends, television programs, soft drink ads, and the guy or girl who is whispering in your ear, it is also natural to get confused about that urge to merge.

Just to set the record straight, no one is saying the desire itself is wrong. Not even God. Particularly not God, for he put the desire there in the first place! However, God had a particular design in mind for the use of that desire, and man doesn't always follow it. That is where the motivation and freedom to choose come in.

Bret's motivation was to fit in. Everyone else was doing it, and he was afraid not to. Little did he know that according to a recent reliable survey, only about 45 percent of kids between fourteen and seventeen answering the survey were actually sexually active. That is far from "everybody."

Most of what Bret took as testimony was actually just talk. The sadder truth is that of the kids in the survey who had had sexual intercourse, 43 percent of the boys and 57 percent of the girls had done so even though they wanted not to. Their reasons? The same as Bret's: peer pressure.

Stacey's motivation was to get attention from guys, to fulfill the desire of the moment, and sometimes to relieve the pressure that was being put on her. Those are all me-centered forces, yet ironically none of them permanently satisfied the basic drive that directs all of us: to avoid anxiety and maintain self-esteem.

Now, if the motivation comes from God, the answers to questions about sex become a little clearer. It is not necessary to become sexually involved with someone just to become acceptable, because you know you are already acceptable in God's eyes. You don't have to give in when you don't want to just to avoid conflict. You realize that being true to the self God has given you eliminates the real conflict and builds self-esteem at the same time.

So when they have played the last slow dance and you are walking toward a dark car with your date, you don't have to worry about doing what is expected of you tonight in the back seat, or saying what is expected of you tomorrow in the locker room. You don't have to be concerned about whether you are a "real man" or a "real woman" and then feel forced to prove it.

You will be just who you are, who God made you to be, and you will do what really feels right for that real you. Believing that God sees you that way and still loves you can take the fear out of looking closely at yourself and making a decision, in any situation.

So—there you have a few bars of the decision process. Love God with everything you have. Then love yourself, and your neighbor just as much as yourself.

Now that you've got the beat, we are sure you can sing the rest for yourself.

4

You Never Listen to Me!

"You just don't understand me!"

Along with "I'm hungry" and "I hate homework," the statement above may be the one most often heard from teenagers.

If you think about it, it can be frustrating, annoying, and downright depressing when no one seems to be able to tune in to how you are feeling. There might be entire days when just about everybody slaps you down with—

"You shouldn't feel that way," or

"Cheer up! These should be the best years of your life," or a flat out,

"You're right! I don't understand you!"

At this point you may be shuddering and wishing we hadn't raked up the memories of those times you would like to forget. Sorry! But we didn't bring this up to plunge you into an immediate blue funk. We just want to show you something you might not be aware of.

You see, the *feeling* that no one understands doesn't automatically mean no one does. It could be that people do understand; they just don't accept. Or perhaps the miserable guy or girl who is feeling misunderstood doesn't understand her/himself, doesn't know how to say what he/she wants to say, or is just plain afraid to say it.

In other words, it is a problem in communication.

At any age, when no one understands or when no one seems to grasp the seriousness of the situation, communication has broken down. It is not just something you have to put up with because you are a teenager. Believe it or not, there are plenty of adults suffering from the same ill! But because of that growing urge to "leave," you may feel it more often than someone in another age bracket, and it may affect you more powerfully.

We are going to introduce you now to two teenagers who had some problems with communication. Their methods of expressing themselves were opposite extremes, so it is possible (even probable) that your way of communicating will fall somewhere between theirs. You will find that out in our quizzes later on. For now, just take a look at Andy and Sara. If you see a glimpse of yourself in either one, heads up!

Sara was so anxious to be unnoticed, she succeeded. That was just about the only thing she did with any expertise.

With her curly auburn hair and big, round, hazel eyes, she had the potential to be not cover-girl beautiful, but striking, interesting. However, she never used her possibilities and instead dressed in faded jeans and baggy T-shirts, wore her hair in an unruly pyramid of frizz, and seldom met anyone's gaze with her eyes.

If her appearance didn't push her completely into the background, her personality gave her the final shove. At school, she was extremely quiet and timid. She ate lunch alone and spent the half hour in the morning between the arrival of her bus and the beginning of her first class in the library, flipping aimlessly through a magazine.

Naturally she had few friends, although she was likable enough. When the other girls in her P.E. class asked her questions about herself, just to be nice, she always smiled and answered, but never volunteered any information. When she had to team up with someone in science lab, she was always eager to get along and do her half of the experiment so they wouldn't think she was a complete idiot, but she only did and said as much as she had to. Most of the time, the other people in her classes couldn't tell you her name. She was just "that real quiet girl with the kind of red hair."

She reacted to her teachers pretty much the same way. She said almost nothing in class and never participated in discussions. When she had to speak—like the time her English teacher assigned a demonstration speech—she did just enough to get by. She spoke for a minute and a half on how to make chocolate chip cookies; under the "D" on her comment sheet, Mr. Stevens wrote that her talk had been "half-baked."

Sara was just as withdrawn at home as she was at school. Her father often commented that she was going through "some weird stage," and her mother usually shrugged it off as being "her age." She spent most of her time in her room, listening to music and drawing sketches which she never finished and always tossed into the wastebasket. If there was homework or chores to do, she invariably waited until the last minute, then charged at it late and did a "half-baked" job.

Inevitably, her parents yelled. Once in a while a teacher would make a remark. In either case, Sara would lower her eyes and withdraw almost physically into her shapeless, safe little shell. It was dull, yes. Yet there were no risks.

But the world is like a giant magnifying glass. Very few people escape its detection forever. Her junior year, a number of things came together that pulled Sara painfully into the open, right where she didn't want to be.

In September a new girl breezed into town. Karen was outgoing and domineering, but very insecure. She was looking for a friend she could shape like a wad of clay. She found such a friend in Sara.

Karen latched on to Sara in study hall the first day of school and, before Sara realized what was happening, they were inseparable. Sara hadn't had a close friend since junior high, and although she did not agree with all of Karen's viewpoints, the relationship became important to her and she did not want to lose it. It was a change having someone to talk to and do things with. Life became a lot less lonely.

However, the friendship was a little lopsided. Karen picked out the movies they saw, the parties they went to, the music they listened to. She decided on everything from the topic of conversation to the topping on their pizza. Sara gagged down a number of anchovies and almost died of boredom at several parties, but that was better than risking the end of the whole thing. She was sure that hearing Karen's account of her endless stream of previous boy-friends for the sixtieth time was better than yawning through the weekends alone in her room. Usually she put her own druthers out of her mind. After all, what did she know about having fun?

Actually, Karen did her two favors. She talked Sara into wearing some make-up, changing her hair, and borrowing a few of her outfits. And then she introduced her to some boys.

Sara had never thought much about guys, probably because the possibility of ever going out with one seemed so remote. So when Karen said she definitely had to pick up on one at the next party or consider herself totally out of it, Sara was terrified. But she put on the old eager-to-please expression and went for it. With some help from Karen, it worked.

Dating Brian turned out to be exactly what Sara expected. She had seen her older sister claw and scratch her way through relationships with boys, so she wasn't surprised when Brian would promise to call and then forget or when he would cancel their dates or show up at her house at odd hours. She liked his sense of humor and he was a good dancer, but to Sara it was not worth the hassle. She checked out of that one.

Eric and Steve were good-looking and took her to neat places, but they expected too much in return physically. She stopped dating both of them, too.

But then there was Kip. If there is such a thing, he was Sara's perfect match. He was fun and witty, but sort of quiet and willing to take things slowly. Sara felt comfortable with him from the start.

Yet she was scared somehow. She was afraid something would happen. It was all too good to be true. Her solution? Don't get too close and you won't get hurt. So as hard as he tried, Kip could not get Sara to open up to him, to let him see who she really was.

For a while there weren't any conflicts. Then everything started to happen at once.

At school, the pressure started from Sara's counselor to decide on some career goals so they could plan her courses for the next year. Sara had absolutely no idea where she was going and frankly had no desire to think about it, so she avoided her counselor like liver and onions. When the counselor called her parents, there was a shouting match at home—her folks shouted and Sara stared at her hands. In the end she rolled her eyes and grudgingly said she would see the counselor. Of course, she didn't.

That Saturday, she had a date with Kip. For some reason she couldn't figure out, he was going to take her to an art show. Well, whatever turned him on was fine.

But Karen had other ideas. Friday afternoon she called Sara and announced that Saturday they were going ice skating. She had a new guy for Sara to meet. Sara had a hard time breaking the news that she had other plans, and when Karen sniffed and said she would be sorry she was dating a wimp like Kip, Sara broke into a cold sweat.

None of that mattered, though, because an hour later Sara's counselor called. Her dad hit the ceiling when he found out Sara hadn't made an appointment to see her. He grounded her for a week.

Sara felt as if she were in a cage, and she saw only two

choices. She could sit on the perch and wait for it all to blow over, or she could take the first opportunity to squeeze between the bars and slip out. She chose the latter, and that night she ran away.

Most of Sara's problems were the result of her failure to communicate. Although Andy was her direct opposite in personality, he suffered from the same ailment. If all adults in Andy's small town had gathered to decide which teenager in the local high school would be most likely to end up in the state penitentiary, Andy would have been their first choice.

With his gleaming crop of thick blonde hair and his crooked smile, Andy wasn't hard to look at. He was tall and broad-shouldered, and he walked like he owned the street, even when he was in completely new surroundings. To the girls in town, he was a fox. To the tougher guys he was a leader. To the rest he was a source of uneasiness. To adults he was obnoxious, demanding, brutal, manipulative, and conniving.

Unlike Sara, Andy thought he knew exactly what he wanted. He should have. He spent half his time thinking about it, and the other half getting it at any cost.

Andy wanted first and foremost to be the leader. He had a crowd of guys who followed him around, none of them candidates for the National Honor Society, to be sure. He made certain they all knew he was boss. If anybody questioned that, they could get lost.

Being Number One meant he couldn't take orders, from anyone. Teachers, principals, and police officers could all forget it if they tried to use their authority. Andy did as he pleased. He also repeated tenth grade twice, had the record for the most school suspensions, and was on probation for driving a car without a license.

Just to be sure everyone knew where he stood, Andy wore all the labels of the self-imposed leader. His usual attire was a tank shirt, a pair of snug jeans, and a tattoo. If he could get away with it he had a cigarette tucked behind his ear. If he couldn't, it was stashed in his sock.

Andy's sentences always came out as demands. Unmet demands were scattered by fists, always cocked and ready. Andy loved a fight, but he liked it better when people did anything to avoid punching it out with him.

With girls, of course, he took a slightly different approach. He wanted women in his life, lots of them, and he had them.

Of course, there were times when he stood them up, broke dates, arrived on their doorsteps drunk, abandoned them for a game of pool, kept them out until three in the morning, and flirted with other girls under their noses. But he usually managed to get out of it while remaining in their good graces.

That is where the Andy charm came in. A few lies, a smooth line, a convincing apology, and the inevitable crooked smile usually did the trick. When it didn't, he brought out the heavy artillery. That's what finally got him into real trouble.

Lisa was fairly new in town, and she was lovely. She was the kind who could wear long straight hair and ruffled blouses even when they were out of style and suddenly have every girl in the school doing it. She gave the appearance of being rather aloof, and that was a challenge for Andy. He had to have her.

His usual, "You're going out with me Saturday" didn't work, so he had to resort temporarily to asking. She finally said yes, and they went out once or twice. He ate lunch with her and met her after classes. She found herself almost liking him, until she ran into his temper.

He was walking her home from school one afternoon, when they stopped at a neighborhood market so Andy could pick up a pack of cigarettes. Lisa wasn't impressed, so she waited impatiently outside. Tony, another boy she had been out with, appeared, and Lisa started talking to him. Just as Tony was asking if she would see a movie with him, Andy walked out. Lisa accepted as quietly as she could, just to be polite to both sides, but Andy came apart. Feeling as if someone had just encroached on his personal territory, he hurled his notebook to the ground and stalked angrily toward Tony.

Tony was not part of Andy's group of cowed followers; he was not one to take orders from what he considered a "punk." When the prefight shoving started, Lisa left the scene in disgust.

Andy arrived at school the next day in an even worse frame of mind. If points had been scored, he would have been named the loser in the fight, and rumor had it that Lisa did not want to see his face again. Andy lined up his group to get even with Tony, and then he set out to look for Lisa. There was no way Andy was ever going to lose.

He did not find Lisa alone until the next afternoon. She was standing on the outside walkway by a second-floor classroom, waiting for a friend. Andy immediately cornered her and turned on the apologetic charm full force. Lisa responded with a cold stare. When Andy crooked his elbow around her neck to bring her closer, she slapped him.

Then he snapped.

Before she realized what was happening, Lisa had been pushed against the railing and was bending backward over the side. Her screams brought teachers and janitors onto the otherwise abandoned walkway in a matter of seconds, but she was plastered, terrified, over the courtyard long enough to bring her parents to the school the next day, threatening Andy with a law suit.

Although it may seem to you that Andy and Sara were just plain messed up, each had a major problem—failure to communicate well. To make that clearer, and to bring it closer to you, let's break it down a little.

First of all, communication involves two factors—someone who relates a message and someone who receives it. To make it even simpler, that means a speaker and a listener. (We are talking here about everyday communication. In the arts, of course, the person with the message to get across can use other means besides speaking.) When you have something to communicate and no one seems to understand, at least part of the responsibility is yours. Maybe, like Sara, you do not always know what you want or are afraid to ask for it. Or perhaps like Andy, you go about saying it the wrong way. It is important to find that out, because it could be bringing you a world of trouble without your even realizing it. Those problems will not stop until you learn to communicate.

Your half of communication—the side with the message to convey—runs deep inside you. Before you can even start learning to express yourself more clearly, you need to make sure the things we've talked about in the previous chapters—positive self-concept and a frame of reference—are at least starting to take shape. Here is why.

Putting your point across involves (1) knowing what your feelings are, and (2) knowing what you want.

Are you actually aware of your feelings, things like anger, fear, excitement? How do you express them, if at all? Being that in touch with yourself requires a strong, positive self-image.

And how do you go about getting what you want? How do you deal with other people's demands? Do you know how to say no? Answering these questions with assurance means having a firm frame of reference for making decisions.

As you can see, both of those areas require a clear knowledge of who you are and a successful method for making decisions. With those two in place, you can go on to learn how to communicate effectively.

Let's start with the first area, your feelings. To get a good grip on it, whip out your pencil and take another quiz.

SELF-SURVEY 4

What Do You Do with Your Feelings?

Below you will find some statements to think about in terms of
you. Read each one, and then write down your first impulse from
the rating given below. Don't mull over any one question, and
when you've put down an answer, let it stand.

> 1   always applies
> 2   often applies
> 3   sometimes applies
> 4   rarely applies
> 5   never applies

Part 1

_____ a.   I am aware that I have feelings (like anger, fear, excitement, sadness, etc.).

_____ b.   When I am afraid (or angry or whatever), other people
seem to notice.

_____ c.   When I am sad (anxious or whatever), I know why.

_____ d.   I do things like slam doors or throw things when I am
angry.

_____ e.   I do things like sing, jump around, or hug people when I
am extremely happy.

_____ f.   I can say to someone, "I feel angry (upset, afraid, on top
of the world) right now."

_____ g.   If I am sad, I have a right to be sad.

Part 2

_____ h.   When I am angry, I say (or at least think) things like, "You
make me mad."

_____ i.   Other people cause me to be unhappy.

_____ j.   If I am sad, I hide it from other people.

_____ k.   If I am afraid, I hide it from other people.

____ l.   If I am angry, I keep it to myself.

____ m. I can talk myself out of being angry.

____ n.   My feelings are pretty unimportant.

____ o.   If I am angry, sad, or afraid, I tell myself, "You shouldn't feel this way."

____ Total for Part 1

____ Total for Part 2

You're probably becoming pretty good at these quizzes by now. If you are, your totals should look something like this: (1) You scored 7 to 18 on Part 1, and 28 to 40 on Part 2; or (2) You scored 25 to 35 on Part 1, and 8 to 20 on Part 2; or (3) You scored 19 to 24 on Part 1, and 21 to 27 on Part 2.

If you fall in group 2, you are quite a bit like Sara in the communication department. For the most part Sara was out of touch with her feelings. She purposely cut herself off from them. For instance, she didn't really like Karen very much, but she was afraid to admit it for fear of being alone again. For that matter, Sara felt lonely 90 percent of the time anyway, but because she did not really know her own feelings, she did nothing to change the loneliness, even when other people tried to help her. It took someone pushy, who had problems of her own she was trying to compensate for, to shove Sara out of the protective shell.

When she did have feelings she could identify, Sara, and perhaps you if you fall into group 2, wasn't sure why she felt them. If you answered with a 4 or 5 on question c, you have no doubt been afraid but couldn't put your finger on the causes. Or total sadness has descended on you for what seemed to be no reason. Sara was that way in her relationship with Kip. He was ideal, but she was scared and didn't know why. Instead of finding out, she just backed off and consequently lost out on something very special.

Group 2 people generally hide from their feelings as if they were going to jump out and grab them! If you identified with Sara, you might try thinking of it this way:

Remember when you were a little kid, alone in your room, trying to go to sleep at night? There were probably times (and, who knows, maybe there still are!) when the pile of clothes you left heaped over a chair looked in the dark an awful lot like a bear, crouched and stalking its prey—you! Or the half-open closet door creaked eerily in the night breeze. What was that! Or a shadow you couldn't identify on the wall suddenly loomed in your imagination as that of the burglar and murderer who was hiding behind your dresser until you were asleep so he could. . . .

At this peak of terror, did you pull the covers over your head and go mad? Or did you lunge for the lamp and flood the room with light, reassuring yourself that it really was only your junk pile, your closet door, and the shadow of the huge stuffed dog your mom moved to the corner when she was cleaning your room?

Refusing to discover what your true feelings really are and to find out where they came from is like sticking your head under the blankets and refusing to come out. You could be hiding from something that is not there to hurt you after all, and you could be driving yourself crazy at the same time!

On the other hand, facing the fears, anxieties (and the joys) squarely is much like reaching up and turning on the light. Exposing those feelings to yourself usually proves that they are not as bad as you feared in that wild imagination of yours. It's okay. You can deal with them. You do not have to hide.

Those in group 2 also have a tendency to think their feelings are not all that important. If you will recall, Sara was annoyed at the fact that Karen made all the decisions, but she never objected because, as she put it, "What do I know about having fun?" She was constantly telling herself, "You shouldn't feel this way, Sara."

But what Sara, and perhaps you, did not realize is that no feeling is irrational, silly, stupid, or unimportant. You have feelings, you have a right to have feelings no matter what they are, and you have a right to consider them important. Remember what we said in Chapter 2 about your being important simply because God made you? Same goes for feelings. God gave us the capacity to feel. When we do, we are using one of his gifts. Shrugging them off as "dumb" is like calling the coastal redwoods or the Atlantic Ocean or "Chicago's" talent "dumb." God made it all. It all has significance.

Finally, Group 2-ers have a tendency to keep what feelings they do own up to locked firmly inside. When Sara's parents got on her case for refusing to get it together for the future, she felt angry and frustrated and crowded, but she never said so. She just lowered her eyes and retreated. And when that no longer protected her, she took off. When you think about it, she had a history of running away. Instead of telling Brian and Eric and Steve how she felt about some of their tricks, she walked away from them. It was too risky to express her feelings. It was easier just to forget it.

So if your score places you in Group 2, you are probably putting across unclear, if not absolutely incorrect, impressions about how you feel. If you don't say, "I'm ticked!" or at least slam a door or hang up the phone, people are likely to think you aren't angry at all and continue to do the things that flip your switch. After all, none of us can be expected to be mind readers.

We would like for you now, Group 2 or not, to zero in on questions "h" and "i." This is a common problem that can happen even with people who know their feelings and think they are important enough to express.

"You make me mad!" people can be heard to say. Or, "You ruined my whole day (prom, homecoming game, or exam week)."

Now, it is true that we react to other people's actions. If they did not do those things, we would not react. When your date cancels out on the Christmas Dance at the last minute or your little brother destroys your Led Zepplin album, you become angry. (Or is that the understatement of the year?) If you are smart, you let him or her know about it. But how you let him or her know is strictly your responsibility, and that's where "You make me so mad" can get you into trouble.

Let's look to Andy for some help on this one. When Lisa didn't respond to his smooth apology system after the scene with Tony, he lost control and could have injured her seriously, if not killed her. He saw nothing wrong with that reaction. After all, she made him mad, and according to him, he could not control that anger. Sure, her response (or lack of it) aroused his temper, but the act of bending her backward over the railing was entirely his. He could also have walked off, burst into tears, or stuck his tongue out at her. The choice was his, not hers.

So much for Group 2. Let's take a look at those who fell into Group 1 on the self survey. Group 1 people are definitely on the other end of the spectrum from those in Group 2, but there are two different ways they can go. Being in Group 1 can be a positive thing, or it can get a person into a heap of trouble.

Believe it or not, Andy could be among the ranks of those in Group 1. He knew how he felt some of the time. The times he didn't we'll discuss later. Often he could not quite admit to himself the real reasons for his feelings. And in every instance when he felt something, he let everybody know about it. So for the most part he was a Group 1.

But so is the person who finds productive ways to express feelings, like Lisa. As soon as she became disgusted with Andy's actions, she made it known that she wanted nothing more to do with him. She didn't fake approval of his smoking or try to bow out gracefully when he wanted to beat up another guy who asked her out.

The difference between the two is that Andy went one step further with his feelings. He used them to manipulate people. When he was angry because a girl told him to back off, he accused her of being a tease and leading him on. A number of girls gave in to that line of reasoning. When he felt frustrated in classes because he lacked the skills, he turned his frustration on the teachers, telling his counselors and parents that his teachers did not give him a fair shake, that they were out to get him.

Knowing your own emotional make-up and using it like a front line on a football team to get where you want to go are definitely two different things. The trick to keeping them separated is to listen for these key phrases, or ones like them, coming from your mouth in moments of anger, fear, or total dejection:

"You always . . ."

"You never . . ."

"If you hadn't . . ."

Even if you don't push people off balconies or get into fist fights, you could be a subtle manipulator. In the communication song, that is strictly off key.

What about Group 3? People in Group 3 are still trying to figure it all out. Sometimes they know what they feel and why, and at other times it's like staring at a test they didn't study for. Sometimes they turn on the light and see their feelings as they really are, and sometimes they hide under the covers. Sometimes they walk right up to parents, friends, dates, and say, in so many words, "I'm angry with you, and I have the right to be." Sometimes they hang up the phone before they are even finished dialing and decide the whole thing is dumb, even when they know it is not. Sometimes they can keep the thing in perspective and stick to how they feel and what they want. Sometimes they can lay a pretty heavy guilt trip on someone.

We see teens in Group 3 as being pretty average. It is not easy to come to grips with feelings, and the person who swings slightly back and forth on the issue is probably just trying to figure it out. Chances are, the guy or girl in Group 3 does pretty well with friends, dates, and casual acquaintances, but still has a hard time dealing with adults, especially parents. That is healthy, but confusing. If you are in Group 3, you might look at it this way: If you can deal with your feelings sometimes, eventually you will be able to do it more. Like all good things (driver's license, graduation, and summer vacation), it will come in time.

One more word before we move on. You may have noticed that in talking about feelings, we have tended to dwell on the less pleasant ones, like anger and fear and the blues. The reason for that is not because we are incurable pessimists, but because as a rule the happier feelings—joy, excitement, contentment—are easy to accept and enjoy and express. It is also not too hard to say to yourself, "Self, you deserve to be happy. This sky-splitting moment belongs to you." Usually when we are happy, we get approval, so we don't hesitate to tell people about it. You have heard the line in songs, for sure, "Nobody wants you when you're down and out," but let your mood be up and you attract people like a rock concert.

However, there are some sad, lonely people who are not even willing to let their happy feelings show. That was the case with Sara. She was a mass of goose bumps inside when she discovered Kip, but she was afraid to let him see it. That was too close for comfort, too revealing.

If you are like Sara in that respect, you are missing out. It might be a good place to start in learning to communicate to let people see your joys. It will make showing your sorrows a lot easier somewhere down the line, when you are ready.

Hopefully at this point, you are convinced that several things about your feelings are important to good communication:

You have to know what your feelings are.

You must consider them to be important.

You need to express them clearly.

You should not use them to manipulate people into giving you what you want.

With all of that intact, you may well now ask, "Okay, then how can I more clearly ask for what I want?" Let's start answering that question by examining the ways you are using now. They may or may not be working, but let's begin by finding out just what they are.

SELF-SURVEY 5

What Do You Do When You Want It Your Way?

Below you will find some statements to think about in terms of you. Read each one and then write down your very first response from the ratings given below. Don't spend too much time on any one question, and don't go back and change any of your answers.

> 1   always applies
> 2   often applies
> 3   sometimes applies
> 4   rarely applies
> 5   never applies

If I ask for what I want and the answer is no, then I:

_____ a.   threaten (ex: "If you don't, I'll never speak to you again").

_____ b.   try to make people feel guilty (ex: "I don't believe this! After all I've done for you!").

_____ c.   offer an "I owe you" (ex: "If you'll do this, I'll do it your way next time").

_____ d.   lie and weasel (ex: say "Okay, I agree with you," and then go off and do it your way anyway).

_____ e.   give reasons for my side (ex: "If you'll just listen, I'll tell you why we should do it my way").

_____ f.   attack the other person's reasons (ex: "That's stupid!").

_____ g.   attack the other person (ex: "You're stupid!").

_____ h.   keep after the person, hoping he or she will give up (ex: "Come on, now, just listen one more time").

_____ i.   give up and get even later (ex: "Okay, forget it, but I'll get you someday!").

_____ j.   figure it wasn't a very reasonable request in the first place (ex: "Never mind. I guess it was dumb of me to even ask").

_____ Total

We will interpret the scores in a minute. But before we go on, we need to talk briefly about that phrase, "Asking for what you want." To some people it may sound a little selfish, bringing to mind the image of a spoiled two-year-old in saggy diapers, stamping his feet and throwing a tantrum.

Unfortunately, an awful lot of people think there is something wrong with trying to get what you want. But as we have said so often, every single person is special and every single person's needs are important. Everyone has the right to go after what they need. God gave you wants just like he gave you a nose. However, a person's way of asking for what he or she wants is often the problem. It is the methods that are selfish, not the needs themselves.

As we interpret the scores from Survey #5, we will explain some of the not-so-swell means. Try to be as honest as you can with yourself about which ones you are using. Then hang in there, and we will explain a way that works a whole lot better.

If you scored between 10 and 25 on the survey, chances are you are not using too many underhanded or damaging methods of communicating (at least the ones we know about!). There may still be room for improvement, so read on, but give yourself a "Great going, kid!" for being a step ahead in the communication section.

Score between 26 and 34? That probably means that from time to time you tend to rely on some of the "tricks" to get things going your way. It does not mean you are a candidate for divorce court or death row. A lot of perfectly nice people are doing it! But definitely read the rest of this chapter very carefully. You will be able to drop those games in favor of something better.

Those of you in the 35 to 50 bracket have tried them all! There is a good possibility you feel lonely, frustrated, or misunderstood a great deal of the time. Don't give up and decide on a career as a hermit. Just read further. It is not as hard as you might think to learn to communicate effectively.

Promises, promises! Let's get on with the positive side: What you can do to get what you want and still maintain good, healthy relationships with the people in your life.

The first step in communicating is to be sure you have the kind of relationship with the person in question that can hold up under a disagreement. When you argue with your brother or sister, do you give each other the iceberg treatment for the next three weeks? Or are you able to agree to disagree?

Are your relationships with your close friends so fragile that they would crumble pitifully if you didn't see eye to eye at all times? Or are they the kind of friendships that grow stronger when you work through problems together?

What about that someone special you may be dating or spending time with? Are you scared to say what you really want from that person for fear the whole thing will disintegrate? Or can you be up front and negotiate without worrying that any minute you are going to find a "Dear John" letter in your locker?

Before communication can work, with parents, friends, fellow siblings, both parties have to be committed to the thing and realize that disagreements are a normal part of every relationship, from the fairy tale romance on down. It has to be more than just an acquaintance the two of you have for convenience. Only when you can both say, "I still like you even if I don't agree with you," will you be able to work out the kinks that are bound to occur.

That was one of Sara's biggest problems. She never dared to disagree with Karen, even though she despised parties, little fish on her pizza, and Karen's choice of clothes. Sara thought that if she spoke her mind in opposition, Karen would walk off and take her friendship with her. As a matter of fact, she probably would, but Sara couldn't see that she would be an awful lot better off without Karen!

She had much the same attitude toward the first few guys she dated. Although she liked some things about Brian, Eric, and Steve, there were minor problems with each one of them. They were things that could have been worked through if Sara had spoken up for her side. But it seemed impossible to her that any relationship could take that, so she just gave up. She actually gave up with Kip, too, by not letting him get close to her. The too-good-to-be-true attitude cost her a super relationship.

Even with her parents Sara had no faith in the durability of human bonds. Although she completely disagreed with the things they yelled at her for, she refused to fight back because she was certain they would toss her out on the sidewalk for life if she did. So she simply shrugged her way through those one-sided discussions. When ignoring them didn't relieve the pressure, she ran away.

You might want to examine your relationships with people and see if they can stand up to the test. If you don't think they can, don't despair. That just means they need a little work, or they might be relationships you want to let go of. There is nothing wrong with that. It doesn't always work out—even in the movies.

Assuming that you do have solid commitments in your relationships, you are ready for the next step. It is simple: ask for anything you want. In the process of communication, there is no such thing as an irrelevant, irrational, unhealthy, sick, crazy, unspiritual, unreasonable, or unfair request! (Sound familiar? It should by now.)

Have you ever asked for something and had your father say, "That's ridiculous!" or your best friend say, "What are you, nuts?" or your date say, "I can't believe you even asked that. That's dumb." At that point, you probably either wanted to chew barbed wire or crawl into the nearest manhole.

But anything you really want is valid, just as any feeling

you have is real. So if you want it, you have the right to ask for it. If someone responds with, "You're being completely unreasonable," that person is in error, not you. If you didn't have your reasons for wanting something, you wouldn't want it!

Because we have all heard that "you're crazy" business, we often temper our requests with what we think the response will be. For example, if a girl knows her parents are going to explode if she asks to be allowed to stay out until 2 A.M., she will ask for midnight instead. Honesty gives way to the fear of being ridiculed or knocked down.

However, the rule says ask for anything you want. If you want to stay out until 2 A.M., say so. If you are told you are out of your ever-loving mind, don't believe it. You are sane, and you are honest as well. Think of it this way: if you ask for only midnight, you may avoid an explosion, but you'll also be miserable at 11:45 when you're heading home wishing you had two more hours. Who knows? They might have said yes.

Now for step three. Do not defend or justify your request. Just state it. "I want to stay out until 2 A.M." Not, "I know it's asking a lot but I'd like to stay out until 2 A.M. tonight because it's prom night and things don't even start picking up until about 11:00 and I've never been late all year blah, blah, blah." No lengthy back-up, please. Just the straight request.

Once that is done, step four takes place. The other person answers. There is at least a 50-50 chance that person will say no. Before you start protesting, remember that the person—parent, boyfriend or best friend since preschool— has the right to say no. The problem with no is that we usually interpret it as "I don't care what you want." But that is not necessarily what it means at all, especially in loving relationships.

For instance, if you tell your date, who happens to be paying that night, that you want to see *Jaws II* at the drive-in, he/she might say, "No way." That doesn't mean he/she could give a hoot less what you want. It may just mean he or she has seen it eight times already, knows it doesn't show as well at a drive-in as at an indoor theater, or is scared out of his or her popcorn by shark movies!

The same goes for parents. Going back to our curfew example, if they turn you down when you try for 2 A.M., that does not necessarily mean they don't want you to have any fun. It could mean they are afraid you will get mugged, or they know what a grouch you are when you do not get enough sleep, or they flat do not want to wait up that late. None of these translates as "I don't care."

But no matter what it means, there you are stuck with no for an answer, right? Not always. According to the next step, the person who says no must now give an acceptable alternative. (Remember, this no-person could be you, so pay attention!)

Under this rule, then, your date must say, "No, I don't want to see *Jaws II* again. But we could go to another theater and catch a different flick."

Dad must say, "No, two o'clock isn't a good idea. Your mother and I would rather have you in by 12:30."

If the tables are turned, *you* must say, "No, I don't like that idea. But how about this?"

You might be scowling at this point and saying, "Great, but how do I get other people to play by these rules?" Well, you might not be able to. All you can do is spell out the system for them and play your part this way. You cannot be responsible for their reactions, but in trying you have nothing to lose and a whole lot to gain.

In the process, there are a couple of things both you and your partner in communication have to stick to. One is that no one is allowed to give reasons. Have you heard yourself saying, "But, Dad! If I come in at 12:30 I'll be the party pooper of the century. Good grief! I can take care of myself. I need to start having some responsibility. . . ." And have your parents shot back with, "Look we have our reasons. There are crazy people on the street at that hour.

And besides, you know how exhausted you'll be when it's time to get up for church in the morning."

Strictly against regulations on either side. That goes for you, too, when you are the one saying no. "Let's go wrap Old Man Wilson's yard in toilet paper," requires only a "No, I don't want to," from you if you really don't want to. There is no need to go into a long explanation of your morals or your lack of cash for the necessary materials. All you owe is an acceptable alternative, like, "Let's go read the magazines in the drugstore instead." The idea is to focus on the alternatives—the "insteads."

Although that may seem confining, think about how much easier it can make certain situations. Picture these:

"No, I don't want to make out. Let's go back to the party."

"Smoke a joint? No thanks. I want to go home."

"No, I'm not into stealing the history exam. I guess I'll just hit the books instead."

Nice and uncomplicated, isn't it?

You see, using debating skills for either the pro or the con gets into some dangerous territory. You start attacking each other's reasons. ("Just because all the other kids are doing it is no reason why you should.") Then you start attacking each other. ("You're just old fashioned. Why don't you look around and see what's happening in the world?") All of which sidetracks the people involved from what they are really after, a mutually acceptable solution. Compare these two conversations and see which one arrives at the desired goal.

Conversation 1

Joe: I want to stay out until 2:00 tonight because it's a big deal. All the other—

Dad: No! Your curfew is 12:30. No exceptions.

Joe: But this is different. The dance isn't even over until
midnight—

Dad: So leave early. There are maniacs on the streets at
that hour and I don't want you out there.

Joe: But that's stupid! I can take care of myself. I'm not a
kid anymore, or haven't you noticed?

Dad: Don't get smart!

Joe: Wake up, Dad! How can I learn responsibility if you
won't give me any?

Dad: You can learn some right now by doing as I say. And
don't argue with me or you won't go at all.

Result: Joe still has to come in at 12:30, and Dad has to
take a dose of his ulcer medicine. Nobody gets what they
want.

Conversation 2

Joe: I want to stay out until 2:00 tonight.

Dad: No. You can come in at 12:30 as usual.

Joe: That's too early. I'd settle for 1:30 even.

Dad: 1:00 and you've got yourself a deal.

Joe: No chance of getting 1:15?

Dad: None.

Joe: Okay. See you at 1:00. But could you be thinking
about extending my curfew permanently?

Dad: We can toss it around, but I'm not making any
promises.

Result: Joe gets a little more time. Dad still has some
peace of mind about Joe's safety. There's hope of future
negotiations.

Number two is obviously the preferable way to go. If
nothing else, it is shorter. It also cuts out name-calling,

shouting, and racking one's brain for good arguments. Sure, there is some discussion. But the focus is on alternatives rather than reasons. In number two, Joe counters with, "Then how about 1:30?" rather than, "Aw, come on, I'm a big boy now." Notice the more positive effect?

The second thing to keep in mind with this system is that once both parties agree to something, it becomes a commitment both must keep. No fair slipping in at 2 A.M. after all. Or taking a "wrong turn" and ending up at *Jaws II* when you've agreed on a pizza and a game of Pac Man. Or trying for just one more kiss when it has been decided you will cool it for the evening. A deal is a deal.

In cases where the negotiated agreement consists of more than one point, you might want to write it down, date it, sign it, and put it where you can both see it—often. Suppose you and your parents have used this communication process to negotiate your curfew, your household chores, and your phone privileges. Perhaps you could jot the following down and hang it on the refrigerator door:

I'll be in by 12:00 on weekends.
I won't ask to go out on school nights.
I'll do the dishes every other night.
I'll wash the car every Saturday.
I'm allowed all the phone calls I want until 9:00 P.M.
I'll allow fifteen-minute intervals between calls.
I'll hang up if Mom or Dad have calls to make.

The agreement should be as binding as a contract, but it can be renegotiated by both parties at any time. The same is true for the verbal agreements. It is okay to call home at 12:00 and say, "Mom, everybody's going out for pizza. Is it okay if I go and stay out 'till 1:00?"

Mom may then say, "No. Get your buns home by 12:30." Or, "Why not grab a coke and get in by 12:45." Or, "Sure, and thanks for checking in."

This clause is kind of an allowance for human error. The

process we are describing requires that a person be completely honest, with himself as well as with others. That takes practice. Sometimes you will fail. So when you realize you have agreed to something that, on second thought, you just cannot accept, go back and see if you can't come up with an agreement you can live with.

Maybe the part about washing the car every Saturday is impossible. You are on the debate team and at least once a month you have a tournament on Saturdays. Could you give up a handful of quarters out of your allowance for Dad to take it to a car wash? Or take out the garbage twice a week instead? Or just knock that out of the agreement completely? Talk it out with the folks and see what you can come up with.

Just be careful that, (1) your renegotiations follow the same process without a bunch of reasons and arguments, and, (2) you don't renegotiate all by yourself! It is not all right to decide at 12:00 that 2:00 was really the only curfew you could live with and then breeze in the door at that hour. That is not renegotiation. That is breach of contract.

One of the beauties of this method is that not only does it get results, fast, but it also shows respect for self and for others. The approaches suggested on Survey #5 don't.

Andy was a master at some of those. Threatening was one of his favorites. He tried to get Tony to stay away from Lisa by promising to knock him out. He even attempted to get Lisa back by using the threat of brute force after his other favorite, persistence, failed. In the process he completely disregarded their rights and made himself look like the bully of the year. In the end, it did not work anyway. Lisa and Tony became a steady item, and Andy lost out completely.

The guilt trip was another one he used, particularly with girls.

"You get all dressed up like that and then you expect me to keep my hands off of you?" he would say. "You led me on on purpose, didn't you?"

Who cared about what the girl wanted?

With adults, he was into the arbitrary decision with a lie as a chaser. "Okay, okay, I'll start going to class," he would say to his counselor, and then he would tell his father, "Those people at that school don't care about me so why should I go to their classes?" That was easier than realizing, and then saying, what he really wanted from school—from life. When it came right down to it, he was not sure of his ability to succeed in school. Pretending not to care was his way of relieving that fear.

Actually, Sara was good at that one, too. She told her parents she would see her counselor about her program just to get them off her case. But then she didn't. She told her counselor she would think about her plans for the future just to get her out of her hair. But then she didn't. Sure, she got in trouble for it eventually, but she seemed to prefer that to telling them all that she was afraid to look at what life had in store for her, because she was afraid it was more of the same!

Sara's negative self-concept also forced her to use the least successful communication tactic of all. That was the old, "Oh, just forget it. I didn't want that anyway" routine. She didn't like three-fourths of the things Karen cooked up, but everytime she would admit it to herself, she would back away from her own wants by saying, "Who am I to argue with her?" While threats, imposed guilt, and even lying might get results sometimes, giving up and browbeating oneself for even having desires never does. Yet it is amazing how many people, like Sara, rely on it.

One thing all of these poor communication methods have in common is, again, lack of respect for self and for the other people involved. Many of the teachings of Christianity point to these very ideas. If nothing else can bring the point home, God can. You might want to reach for your Bible again and take a look at some passages that provide a perfect background for communication.

One is Romans 12:10. Here Paul says, "Be kindly affectioned one to another with brotherly love; in honour preferring one another." He also wrote to the Philippians (2:3), "Let each esteem other better than themselves." Peter, too, said, "Honor all men. Love the brotherhood."

So it is important to take other people's needs and feelings into consideration in communicating. Otherwise, you end up like Andy.

Andy's parents managed to get him off the hook legally for his attack on Lisa, but he was expelled from the school for the rest of the year. The school arranged for some special counseling, but Andy was too tied up in his communication techniques to let that help him. When school started the next year, it just didn't seem worthwhile to go back. Equipped with a negative self-concept, one frame of reference (himself), and a sack full of "tricks," he left home—but only physically. Plagued by the fear that he really wasn't going to make it, he didn't. As far as we know, life is still a series of meaningless jobs, empty relationships, rootless places. As ruthlessly as he tries, he will never get what he wants as long as communication means only Andy to Andy.

Christianity deals with the other side of this thing, too—knowing your own mind and sticking to your feelings and convictions as well as caring about other people. That might seem a little contradictory when you think about all the references in the Bible to loving other people better than yourself and always putting others first, second only to God himself. But a look at 2 Thessalonians 2:2 might clear that up.

In his letter to the Thessalonians, Paul says, basically, don't let anybody change your mind or confuse you. If indeed you believe that God created you in his image and therefore you are special, and if the teachings of Christ form the basis for your frame of reference, then your needs and the things you want will be things you have the right to ask for.

Let's go back to Sara and see how this fits in.

Sara was away from home less than two hours when she realized running away was not the answer, so she slithered back. That particular incident had been blown completely out of proportion, but her mother was concerned enough to take her in for counseling. For Sara, it worked.

Once convinced that she was with people she could trust, Sara first began to learn some things about herself. She discovered she had a talent for art (something Kip had seen right away) and decided to pursue it as a possible career or at least as a serious hobby.

She figured out that she did need friends, but friends who liked her as she was, who didn't push and pull until she was no longer recognizable. Those two lessons alone transformed her into the real Sara.

Eventually she learned to like herself and trust the feelings she had: feelings of anger when boys treated her shabbily or when Karen tried to run her life; feelings of being trapped by her parents who had her locked into "that awful period of being a teenager." Finally, certain that those feelings and wants were valid simply because she was made by God and was therefore allowed to have them, she learned to do something about them.

First, she started standing up to Karen. As expected, Karen dropped out of her life as if a trap door had been opened under her. But Sara was able to make several new friends while painting the sets for the school musical. They were better friends, real friends, who let her pick the movies and the pepperoni and the subject of discussion just as often as they did.

She thought she had lost Kip, who had decided she was "messed up" and had broken up with her soon after she ran away. That hurt, but she dated some other guys and managed to stand up for her rights when conflicts arose. Some of them liked it, some of them did not. But about a year after he backed out of the picture, Kip came back into it. The Sara he had seen glimpses of had emerged totally, and he was crazy about her.

Working things out with her parents was tougher. Painfully, she talked them into a written agreement for her household jobs, curfews, and general attitudes on both sides. Her father was never able to stick to it. He saw it as a bunch of ridiculous nonsense.

But Sara and her mother found that list magnetically attached to the refrigerator door to be the best thing that ever happened to their relationship. Sure, they tossed renegotiations back and forth in voices loud enough for the neighbors to take in, but the results were almost always positive. They communicated, and both sides "won." The confidence Sara gained through that carried over into most of her other dealings with people.

Of course, that process took a long time, over a year. But now Sara is about to graduate from high school. She has a job lined up as a girl Friday in an advertising firm, and she is registered for art courses at the community college at night. She thinks she is serious about Kip, but she wants to take it slowly. With some real anxiety on both sides, they have agreed to date other people if the opportunity comes up. Sara and her mother are close, but she and her father have settled into a cold coexistence. All the problems have not been solved, but there is progress still being made for Sara.

If she keeps communicating, and if you do, any conflict can be dealt with. It just means, (1) remembering that there will be bumps along the way no matter what; (2) knowing what you feel about them; (3) saying what you feel; (4) asking for what you want; and (5) negotiating on fair ground.

That is the song on paper. The singing only comes with practice.

5

Go for It!

"You call that music?"

"What in the world kind of dance is THAT?"

"Turn that thing down—please!"

Those are familiar words to you, no? Well, it may come as a surprise, but your generation is not the first to have those sentiments hammered into its ears.

Teens in the twenties—your grandparents, possibly—cranked up their phonographs and did the Charleston, to the dismay of their parents.

Forties teenagers jitterbugged the night away and drove their folks to distraction with the jumping sound of the Big Bands. Your parents, perhaps.

From the night Elvis first shocked America's older generation by swiveling his hips on the Ed Sullivan Show, teens in the fifties went wild over rock'n roll. Those are the same mild-mannered adults who may be teaching you transitive verbs and simultaneous equations today!

The point is that teenagers have long been known for the same set of basic characteristics, expressed in the music they listen to constantly. Since the first adolescent felt his first leaving pang, people between thirteen and eighteen have been pulling away from the trappings of childhood and feverishly clinging to them at the same time.

In the process, they have all struggled with their self-concepts, tangled with their frames of reference, and agonized over their need to communicate. Some, like Bonnie and Lyle, Stacey and Bret, Sara and Andy, have run into some heavy-duty problems in the process. Some have walked through it with fewer tumbles and spills. Some have probably been an awful lot like you. None have breezed through without a ripple.

Yet most of those millions of teens who clawed, scratched, bit, laughed, cried, and prayed their way through the leaving process made it. They learned who they were, decided what they wanted, and figured out how to let everyone else know both. They became happy, productive adults who traveled into adulthood without being dragged down by the extra baggage of wanting to break away and wanting to stay. They "left."

You, with your New Wave music, your "Pogo" dance, your rock star T-shirts and designer jeans will be no different. You, too, will bring together those three parts of a well-balanced person we have been talking about. Like all the dancing, singing, rocking teenagers before you, you will shake off the dilemma of going vs. staying. In time, you, too, will be ready. You will begin leaving.

Now notice we said "you will *begin leaving.*" Remember that leaving is a process, like growing. We hope you have come to think of it as a journey, rather than a destination. Although the special problems of being fourteen or sixteen will pass away as you get your act together, and you will physically leave home to go out on your own, you will never stop developing. You will always have something to work on.

Don't look so depressed! That can be an exciting prospect if you know yourself well enough to see what to work on. Let us prove it to you. Break out that pencil again, and take one last self survey.

SELF-SURVEY 6

Where Are You in the Leaving Process Now?

Below you will find eighteen statements about situations you may be facing now. Read them carefully and decide how, if at all, they apply to you.

Beside each one you will see three blanks. If the statement is true for you, put a check in the first blank. If the statement is false for you, put a check in the second blank. Whether the statement is true or false, if it is also a problem for you, put a check in the third blank also.

T   F   P

____ ____ ____ 1. The people I hang around with drink and/or smoke marijuana.

____ ____ ____ 2. When I go out on a date, I don't know how to make my date feel relaxed and comfortable with me.

____ ____ ____ 3. I get jealous a lot.

____ ____ ____ 4. I have few dates compared to other people my age.

____ ____ ____ 5. My parents won't let me stay out as late as I want to.

____ ____ ____ 6. I don't think you should have sex relations before marriage.

____ ____ ____ 7. I want to date people in groups that don't accept me.

____ ____ ____ 8. My friends don't listen to what I have to say.

____ ____ ____ 9. My friends want me to go steady.

____ ____ ____ 10. I fall in love with everyone I go out with.

____ ____ ____ 11. I have no one to discuss problems with.

____ ____ ____ 12. I'm not allowed to date people who don't go to my church.

____ ____ ____ 13. Dating makes me nervous.

——— ——— ——— 14. My feelings are always getting hurt.

——— ——— ——— 15. I let the people I'm with decide where we'll go and what we'll do.

——— ——— ——— 16. I'm not as good-looking as most of my friends.

——— ——— ——— 17. My parents embarrass me and treat me like a child in front of my friends.

——— ——— ——— 18. I don't always want to kiss a date good night.

There are no right or wrong responses to the statements you just answered. What we are going to focus on are the statements for which you checked the third column, "This is a problem." Those are the areas where you haven't quite fit all the pieces together yet. They are the things you will work to become stronger in as you go through the leaving process. Let's take a look at those.

Did you have two or more "problem" blanks checked on questions 3, 4, 7, 10, 13, and 16? If so, that means you still have some doubts about self-concept. Maybe you aren't quite sure who you are yet, or whether you like what you see when you look in the mirror. You might want to go back and read Chapter 2 again. Developing a positive self-concept should really be at the top of your list of things to do.

Did you check two or more of the "problem" blanks on questions 1, 6, 9, 12, 15, and 18? If yes, then it is a pretty safe bet that your frame of reference isn't set up quite the way you want it. Maybe you still have trouble making decisions you're satisfied with. We suggest giving Chapter 3 another look. As you move toward leaving, you will want to zero in on your system of values.

Did you check that important third column for two or more of statements 2, 5, 8, 11, 14, and 17? If that is the case, communication problems are probably a drag for you right now. Perhaps you are fighting with your folks a great deal or are feeling more misunderstood than Charlie Brown himself. Further examination of Chapter 4 could relieve some of that for you. With the leaving process going full force in your life, some concentration on making your wants known will pay off.

If you are not as strong as you need to be in just one of those three areas, the future looks hopeful for you. It will not be hard to get the kinks out of that one knotty area.

Even if two of our big three are wobbly—you can maintain relationships just fine but you are not happy with yourself, or you have everything you want but feel no one likes you—you are still going to be okay. At least you have learned to "get strong" in one area. The other two won't be impossible to lick. Sure, you have your work cut out for you. But it is going to be exciting work, if you think of it the way any artist looks at the process of creating.

Like the members of a rock band—or a movie producer or a painter or (oh, yes!) a writer—you will sweat, cry, and buckle with frustration. But when you are there, when you finally get it right, the genuine satisfaction will be like nothing you have ever heard before. You will get the sound you want; other people will hear it; you will feel satisfied.

We cannot leave you without asking you to fan through your Bible just once more, for some parting words of encouragement. Let the pages fall to Romans 8:28, 38–39. There Paul says to us, "And we know that all things work together for good to them that love God, to them who are the called according to his purpose." "For I am persuaded, that neither death, nor life, nor angels, nor principalities, nor powers, nor things present, nor things to come, nor height, nor depth, nor any other creature, shall be able to separate us from the love of God, which is in Christ Jesus our Lord."

How can you go wrong? Even when things fall into a hopeless heap—as no doubt they will seem to sometimes— your unconditional love for God and his for you will guarantee that it will all "work together for good."

So go for it! No doubt, you are *going* to be a hit!